Blackstone's
Police Q&A
Road Traffic 2005

Blackstone's
Police Q&A

Road Traffic 2005

Third edition

Huw Smart and John Watson

OXFORD
UNIVERSITY PRESS

OXFORD
UNIVERSITY PRESS

Great Clarendon Street, Oxford OX2 6DP
Oxford University Press is a department of the University of Oxford.
It furthers the University's objective of excellence in research, scholarship,
and education by publishing worldwide in

Oxford New York

Auckland Bangkok Buenos Aires Cape Town Chennai
Dar es Salaam Delhi Hong Kong Istanbul Karachi Kolkata
Kuala Lumpur Madrid Melbourne Mexico City Mumbai Nairobi
São Paulo Shanghai Taipei Tokyo Toronto

Oxford is a registered trade mark of Oxford University Press
in the UK and certain other countries

Published in the United States
by Oxford University Press Inc., New York
A Blackstone Press Book

© Huw Smart and John Watson 2005

The moral rights of the authors have been asserted

Database right Oxford University Press (maker)

Crown copyright material is reproduced under Class Licence Number C01P0000148
with the permission of HMSO and the Queen's Printer for Scotland

All rights reserved. No part of this publication may be reproduced,
stored in a retrieval system, or transmitted, in any form or by any means,
without the prior permission in writing of Oxford University Press,
or as expressly permitted by law, or under terms agreed with the appropriate
reprographics rights organization. Enquiries concerning reproduction
outside the scope of the above should be sent to the Rights Department,
Oxford University Press, at the address above

You must not circulate this book in any other binding or cover
and you must impose the same condition on any acquirer

British Library Cataloguing in Publication Data

Data available

Library of Congress Cataloging in Publication Data

Data available

ISBN 0-19-926835-5

10 9 8 7 6 5 4 3 2 1

Typeset by SNP Best-set Typesetter Ltd., Hong Kong
Printed in Great Britain
on acid-free paper by
Ashford Colour Press Limited, Gosport, Hampshire

Contents

Introduction	ix
New to Blackstone's Police Q&As for 2005	xi
Acknowledgements	xiii

1 Classifications and Concepts — 1
Study preparation — 1
Questions — 1
Answers — 11

2 Offences Involving Standards of Driving — 20
Study preparation — 20
Questions — 20
Answers — 29

3 Notices of Intended Prosecution — 38
Study preparation — 38
Questions — 38
Answers — 41

4 Accidents and Collisions — 44
Study preparation — 44
Questions — 44
Answers — 48

5 Drink Driving — 52
Study preparation — 52
Questions — 52
Answers — 68

Contents

6	**Insurance**	**83**
	Study preparation	83
	Questions	83
	Answers	87

7	**Safety Measures**	**90**
	Study preparation	90
	Questions	90
	Answers	94

8	**Other Measures Affecting Safety**	**98**
	Study preparation	98
	Questions	98
	Answers	105

9	**Construction and Use**	**111**
	Study preparation	111
	Questions	111
	Answers	117

10	**Traffic Signs and Directions**	**121**
	Study preparation	121
	Questions	121
	Answers	124

11	**Driver Licensing**	**126**
	Study preparation	126
	Questions	126
	Answers	133

12	**Excise and Registration**	**139**
	Study preparation	139
	Questions	139
	Answers	144

13	**Goods and Passenger Vehicles**	**148**
	Study preparation	148
	Questions	148
	Answers	155

14	**Fixed Penalty System**	**161**
	Study preparation	161
	Questions	161
	Answers	165
15	**Pedal Cycles**	**168**
	Study preparation	168
	Questions	168
	Answers	171
16	**Forgery and Falsification of Documents**	**173**
	Study preparation	173
	Questions	173
	Answers	175
	Question Checklist	**177**

Introduction

Before you get into the detail of this book, there are two myths about multiple choice questions (MCQs) that we need to get out of the way right at the start:

1. that they are easy to answer;
2. that they are easy to write.

Take one look at a professionally designed and properly developed exam paper such as those used by the Police Promotion Examinations Board or the National Board of Medical Examiners in the US and the first myth collapses straightaway. Contrary to what some people believe, MCQs are not an easy solution for examiners and not a 'multiple-guess' soft option for examinees.

That is not to say that *all* MCQs are taxing, or even testing — in the psychometric sense. If MCQs are to have any real value at all, they need to be carefully designed and follow some agreed basic rules.

And this leads us to myth number 2.

It is widely assumed by many people and educational organisations that anyone with the knowledge of a subject can write MCQs. You need only look at how few MCQ writing courses are offered by training providers in the UK to see just how far this myth is believed. Similarly, you need only to have a go at a few badly designed MCQs to realise that it *is* a myth nonetheless. Writing bad MCQs is easy; writing good ones is no easier than answering them!

As with many things, the design of MCQs benefits considerably from time, training and experience. Many MCQ writers fall easily and often unwittingly into the trap of making their questions too hard, too easy or too obscure, or completely different from the type of question that you will eventually encounter in your own particular exam. Others seem to use the MCQ as a way to catch people out or to show how smart they, the authors, are (or think they are).

There are several purposes for which MCQs are very useful. The first is in producing a reliable, valid and fair test of knowledge and understanding across a wide range of subject matter. Another is an aid to study, preparation and revision for such examinations and tests. The differences in objective mean that there are slight

Introduction

differences in the rules that the MCQ writers follow. Whereas the design of fully validated MCQs to be used in high stakes examinations which will effectively determine who passes and who fails have very strict guidelines as to construction, content and style, less stringent rules apply to MCQs that are being used for teaching and revision. For that reason, there may be types of MCQ that are appropriate in the latter setting which would not be used in the former. However, in developing the MCQs for this book, the authors have tried to follow the fundamental rules of MCQ design but they would not claim to have replicated the level of psychometric rigour that is — and has to be — adopted by the type of examining bodies referred to above.

These MCQs are designed to reinforce your knowledge and understanding, to highlight any gaps or weaknesses in that knowledge and understanding and to help focus your revision of the relevant topics.

I hope that we have achieved that aim.

Good luck!

New to Blackstone's Police Q&As for 2005

References to Blackstone's Police Manuals

For 2005, every answer is followed by a paragraph reference to Blackstone's Police Manuals. This means that once you have attempted a question and looked at an answer, the Manual can immediately be referred to for help and clarification.

Unique numbers for each question

Each question and answer has been given the same unique number. This should ensure that there is no confusion as to which question is linked to which answer. For example, Question 2.1 is linked to Answer 2.1

Checklists

The checklists are designed to help you keep track of your progress when answering the multiple choice questions. If you fill in the checklist after attempting a question, you will be able to check how many you got right on the first attempt and will know immediately which questions need to be revisited a second time.

Acknowledgements

This book has been written as an accompaniment to *Blackstone's Police Manuals*, and will test the knowledge you have accrued through reading that series. It is of the essence that full study of the relevant chapters in each *Police Manual* is completed prior to attempting the Questions and Answers. As qualified police trainers we recognise that students tend to answer questions incorrectly either because they don't read the question properly, or because one of the 'distracters' has done its work. The distracter is one of the three incorrect answers in a multiple choice question (MCQ) and is designed to distract you from the correct answer, and in this way discriminate between candidates: the better-prepared candidate not being 'distracted'.

So particular attention should be paid to the *Answers* sections, and students should always ask themselves, 'Why did I get that question wrong?' and, just as importantly, 'Why did I get that question right?'. Combining the information gained in the *Answers* sections together with re-reading the chapter in the *Police Manual* should lead to a greater understanding of the subject matter.

The authors wish to thank Katie at Oxford University Press for her support, patience and cajoling skills! Thanks also to Geraldine Mangley for her invaluable assistance. We would also like to show our appreciation to Alistair MacQueen for his vision and support, without which this project would never have been started.

Huw would like to thank both Julie and their beautiful baby Hâf, for their constant strength and support during long evenings and weekends of writing, when he could have been having fun with the family.

John would like to thank Sue for her support; also David, Catherine and Andrew for not too many, 'Dad, can I have . . .'.

1 | Classifications and Concepts

STUDY PREPARATION

The classifications and concepts set out in road traffic legislation are critical to understanding and proving many — if not all — the relevant offences. There is little point in knowing that a particular offence can only be committed by a motor vehicle for instance, if you don't recognise a 'motor vehicle' when you come across one. It should be noted that the Police Reform Act 2002 has added another definition of a 'motor vehicle' to the one more commonly found in s. 185(1) of the Road Traffic Act 1988.

The classifications and concepts addressed in this chapter are therefore the building blocks for the rest of the subjects that follow — so they are well worth careful study.

QUESTIONS

Question 1.1

Section 59 of the Police Reform Act 2002 contains its own definition of a 'motor vehicle'. Which of the below would be the correct description of a motor vehicle under this Act?

A Any mechanically propelled vehicle, which is intended or adapted for use on roads.
B Any mechanically propelled vehicle, whether or not it is intended or adapted for use on roads.
C Any mechanically propelled vehicle, which is intended for use on roads.
D Any vehicle whose function is to be used on roads as a mechanically propelled vehicle.

1

1. Classifications and Concepts

Question 1.2

ARMSTRONG owns a vintage car, which he takes to shows, by loading it onto a trailer and towing it. The vintage car was manufactured in 1939, and was used on the road until 1970. ARMSTRONG, however, has never used the car on the road since he bought it.

Could ARMSTRONG's car be described as a motor vehicle, under s. 185(1) of the Road Traffic Act 1988, in these circumstances?

A No, as the vehicle is not currently being used on the road.
B Yes, but only if ARMSTRONG intends to use the vehicle on the road in future.
C Yes, regardless of ARMSTRONG's intent as to the future use of the vehicle.
D No, as ARMSTRONG has not adapted the vehicle for use on roads.

Question 1.3

NEWBERRY removed the engine from his car, and arranged for his friend, SIMMONDS to help him tow the car to a garage to have a new engine fitted. They were stopped by the police while towing the car on a road.

Which of the following statements is correct, in relation to the status of the vehicle under the Road Traffic Act 1988?

A It was both mechanically propelled and a motor vehicle.
B It was still mechanically propelled, but was not a motor vehicle.
C It was still a motor vehicle, but was not mechanically propelled.
D It was neither a motor vehicle nor mechanically propelled.

Question 1.4

The definition of a 'mechanically propelled vehicle' is important, when determining whether or not a vehicle is in fact a 'motor vehicle', under the Road Traffic Act 1988.

In relation to the term 'mechanically propelled vehicle', which of the following statements is correct?

A An electrically assisted pedal cycle will qualify as a 'mechanically propelled vehicle'.
B A motor-assisted pedal cycle will be a 'mechanically propelled vehicle', even when it is being pedalled.
C A petrol-driven micro-scooter will not qualify as a 'mechanically propelled vehicle'.

D A motor-assisted pedal cycle will not be a 'mechanically propelled vehicle', when it is being pedalled.

Question 1.5

In relation to the definition of a 'passenger vehicle', which of the following statements, if either, is correct?
1. If a vehicle has been adapted to carry passengers and their effects, as well as goods, it will still be a 'passenger vehicle'.
2. If a passenger vehicle is constructed to carry more than 8 but no more than 16 passengers, it will be classed as a 'mini-bus'.

A Statement 1 only.
B Statement 2 only.
C Both statements.
D Neither statement.

Question 1.6

In respect of the definition of a 'medium-sized goods vehicle' (including its permissible weight and the number of passengers it may carry), which of the following statements is correct?

A More than 3 tonnes, no more than 9 passengers including the driver.
B More than 3.5 tonnes, no more than 9 passengers excluding the driver.
C More than 3.5 tonnes, no limit on the number of passengers.
D More than 3.5 tonnes, no more than 9 passengers including the driver.

Question 1.7

Section 108(1) of the Road Traffic Act 1988 defines a 'moped'. In respect of a 'moped' first used after 1 August 1977, which of the following statements is correct?

A It must have an engine size that does not exceed 125 cc and a maximum speed of 50 kilometres per hour.
B It must have an engine size that does not exceed 50 cc and be fitted with pedals.
C It must have an engine size that does not exceed 50 cc and a maximum speed of 50 kilometres per hour.
D It must have an engine size that does not exceed 50 cc and be propelled by electric power.

1. Classifications and Concepts

Question 1.8

LEES had been involved in a long-standing dispute with her neighbour, GREEN, over parking outside their houses. One morning, LEES was leaving for work. However, GREEN had parked his car bumper to bumper with her own, making it difficult for her to get out of her parking space. LEES deliberately drove into GREEN's car to try to move it forward, to give herself some space. As a result, damage was caused to both vehicles.

In these circumstances, what test would a court have to apply, in determining whether an 'accident' has taken place, under the Road Traffic Act 1988?

A That an ordinary person would think an accident has taken place.
B None. An accident has not taken place, as the act was deliberate.
C That LEES realised at the time that an accident was taking place.
D That a reasonable person would think an accident has taken place.

Question 1.9

CLIFFORD was driving his car and his wife LISA was in the front passenger seat. CLIFFORD's mobile phone rang, but it had fallen behind his seat. CLIFFORD asked LISA to steer the car while he reached for his phone. LISA took hold of the wheel, but the car veered across the carriageway and collided with a lamp post, causing substantial damage to it.

Who may be charged in relation to 'driving' in these circumstances?

A LISA is not liable, as only one person may be the driver of a vehicle at any one time.
B LISA and CLIFFORD could both be held to be the driver of the vehicle.
C LISA and CLIFFORD could both be held to be the driver of the vehicle, provided they are not charged with dangerous driving.
D Either LISA or CLIFFORD could be held to be the driver, but to charge both is not permitted in relation to road traffic offences.

Question 1.10

MICHAELS was driving his car on a road when his mobile phone rang. He did not have a hands-free kit, therefore he stopped at the side of the road. MICHAELS answered the phone while his car was stationary, with the engine still running. The handbrake was unset and MICHAELS was controlling the vehicle with the footbrake. He remained in this position for 10 minutes, before completing the call and driving off.

In these circumstances, would MICHAELS have been the driver of the motor vehicle, while it was stationary?

A No, as the vehicle was stationary, he was no longer a driver.
B Yes, he will be a driver until the end of his journey.
C Yes, because he was controlling the propulsion of the vehicle with the footbrake.
D No, the vehicle was stationary only for a short period of time.

Question 1.11

In which of the following scenarios will the person probably **not** be deemed to be 'driving' a vehicle?
1. McDONAGH was pushing his car, while leaning through the window to steer it.
2. GUNNEL was sitting astride his motorbike and was pushing it along with both feet.
3. JONES was the front seat passenger in a car and grabbed the steering wheel suddenly to stop the driver hitting a cat.

A All three scenarios.
B None of the above scenarios.
C Scenarios 1 and 3 only.
D Scenario 2 only.

Question 1.12

KELLY was drunk and decided to drive home. KELLY opened his car door and sat in the driver's seat. However, when he tried to start the car, KELLY could not do so because he was using his house keys. Eventually KELLY managed to find the correct key, but the car would not start, as the battery was flat.

In these circumstances, which would be the first point at which KELLY has 'attempted' to drive his car?

A He did not attempt to drive the car at any time.
B When he tried to start the car with the correct key.
C When he first sat in the driver's seat.
D When he tried to start the car with the house key.

1. Classifications and Concepts

Question 1.13

WATKINS borrowed his friend's car one evening and went out drinking. On his way home, he went to a takeaway restaurant. WATKINS was overheard by CARTER, boasting about driving home. It was obvious that WATKINS was drunk and CARTER telephoned the police. WATKINS was leaving the premises when the police arrived.

In relation to the proof required to establish whether a person is 'in charge' of a vehicle, which of the following is true?

A WATKINS must show that there was no likelihood of him resuming control of the vehicle while he was drunk.
B The prosecution must show that WATKINS intended to drive the vehicle in the future.
C WATKINS must show that he had no intention of resuming control of the vehicle while he was drunk.
D The prosecution must show that there was a likelihood of WATKINS driving the vehicle in the future.

Question 1.14

HILTON took his car to MOHAMMED's garage for repairs. About five minutes after HILTON left, MOHAMMED had to park the car in the road to make room for another car. As MOHAMMED was walking away from the car, Constable DAVIES was walking past and noticed that it was not displaying a vehicle excise licence.

Who would be the 'keeper' of the vehicle in these circumstances?

A HILTON only, as he is the owner of the vehicle.
B MOHAMMED only.
C Neither, as the vehicle was not on the road for long.
D Both MOHAMMED and HILTON.

Question 1.15

HAWKINS was involved in a road traffic collision. HAWKINS was to blame, having travelled through a red traffic light. When the police arrived, HAWKINS told the officer that she was diabetic and had blacked out momentarily, having suffered a hypoglycaemic episode.

Would HAWKINS be able to rely on this as a defence in these circumstances?

A No, HAWKINS has no defence in these circumstances.
B Yes, such an attack would provide an automatic defence.

1. Classifications and Concepts

C Yes, provided she could show the attack was unforeseen.
D No, even though the element of mens rea is not present, the actus reus is.

Question 1.16

In which of the following scenarios, if either, will the vehicle be 'on a road' as defined by s. 192(1) of the Road Traffic Act 1988?
1. RANDALL parked his van on his driveway; however, the rear of the vehicle was sticking out and blocking the pavement.
2. LANG was seen riding a motorcycle without a helmet, on a public bridleway.

A Scenario 1 only.
B Scenario 2 only.
C Both scenarios.
D Neither scenario.

Question 1.17

Case law has often assisted in deciding whether or not a car park may become a 'road' in certain circumstances.

In relation to whether a car park can become a 'road' for the purposes of the Road Traffic Act 1988, which of the following statements is correct?

A A car park is provided for parking vehicles and could not be a road in any circumstances.
B A car park forms part of the highway; therefore will always be a road for the purposes of the Act.
C A car park is provided for parking vehicles and could only be a road in exceptional circumstances.
D A car park with road markings and traffic signs will always be a road, if it has the general appearance of a road.

Question 1.18

VIVIER arranged a Scout fête, and was given permission to use a field belonging to GILES, a local farmer. On the day of the fête, entry was restricted to members of the local Scout groups, and drivers of vehicles were charged £1 each for entry.

In relation to road traffic offences, would GILES' field qualify as a 'public' place in these circumstances?

A No, as entry to the field was restricted to certain people.

1. Classifications and Concepts

B Yes, as members of the public were allowed access.
C Yes, people were using the field with GILES' permission.
D No, as the people using the field were charged for entry.

Question 1.19

TANNER was stopped by Constable CHEN one evening as she drove her vehicle in an access road leading to a block of flats. Constable CHEN suspected that TANNER had been drinking and asked her to supply a specimen of breath, which proved positive. She was later charged with driving with excess alcohol. At a later court appearance, she pleaded not guilty. TANNER relied on the defence that the access road which she was driving on belonged to a local housing department and that it was not a public place. There were signs at the entrance to the access road saying 'Private Residents Only'.

What would the prosecution need to show, in order to prove that the road was, in fact, a public place?

A The prosecution would need to provide clear evidence that the road was used by motorists other than residents.
B The prosecution would not be able to show that the access road was a public place, because of the signs that were in place.
C The prosecution would need to provide some evidence that the road was used by motorists other than residents.
D The prosecution would not be able to show that the access road was a public place, because a private place cannot become a public place in any circumstances.

Question 1.20

In relation to the term 'public place', which of the following statements, if either, is/are correct?

1. It will be for the defence to prove that a place is not a 'public place', in cases where a dispute arises.
2. For a public place to be converted into a private place, a physical obstruction must be in place to prevent general entry.

A Statement 1 only.
B Statement 2 only.
C Both statements.
D Neither statement.

1. Classifications and Concepts

Question 1.21

BAKER was driving a tractor and towing a trailer laden with hay on a road, on behalf of his employer, RICHARDSON. Constable SHAH stopped BAKER for having an insecure load, as some of the bales fell off the trailer and on to the road. Constable SHAH reported BAKER for the offence and later spoke to RICHARDSON, who denied responsibility as BAKER had loaded the trailer himself. RICHARDSON stated he would not have authorised the load to be carried in such a manner.

Would RICHARDSON be guilty of 'using' a vehicle in these circumstances?

A No, as he did not authorise BAKER to use the vehicle in such a way.
B No, as BAKER was not acting in the course of his employment.
C No, as BAKER was drawing a trailer, only he could 'use' it.
D Yes, he would be guilty in these circumstances alone.

Question 1.22

In relation to the term 'using' a vehicle, which of the following statements, if either, is/are correct?
1. If a vehicle is on a road and is in an unroadworthy condition, the owner cannot be said to be using it.
2. The passenger in a vehicle cannot be guilty of using it in any circumstances.

A Statement 1 only.
B Statement 2 only.
C Both statements.
D Neither statement.

Question 1.23

PRICE is the transport manager of a haulage company. He knows that most of his drivers make false entries on their tachograph sheets. PRICE has not instructed them to do this, but as it means that the drivers work longer hours on behalf of the company, he does not stop them. HILLMAN, the owner of the company, is unaware of what is happening.

Is either PRICE or HILLMAN guilty of 'causing' offences in relation to drivers' hours in these circumstances?

A Yes, PRICE only, as he has turned a blind eye to what is happening.
B No, neither person is guilty of 'causing' offences in these circumstances.
C Yes, HILLMAN only as the owner of the company.
D Yes, both people would be 'causing' offences in these circumstances.

1. Classifications and Concepts

Question 1.24

Generally, in order to prove an offence of 'permitting', it will be necessary to show some knowledge by the defendant of the use of his or her vehicle.

What must you prove the defendant knew in order for him or her to be guilty of 'permitting'?

A Knowledge only that the vehicle was being used on a road.
B Knowledge by the defendant of the vehicle's use or of the unlawful nature of that use.
C Knowledge only by the defendant of the vehicle's use.
D Knowledge by the defendant of the vehicle's use and of the unlawful nature of that use.

1. Classifications and Concepts

ANSWERS

Answer 1.1

Answer **B** — The definition of a motor vehicle under s. 59 of the Police Reform Act 2002 is, '*any mechanically propelled vehicle, whether or not it is intended or adapted for use on roads*'. This section created an offence of using a motor vehicle in a manner which is likely to cause harassment, alarm or distress to members of the public. The key difference between this definition and the one contained in s. 185(1) of the Road Traffic Act 1988 is that it is irrelevant whether the mechanically propelled vehicle was intended or adapted for use on the road (which about covers any vehicle capable of being propelled mechanically). Answers A and C are therefore incorrect. The description contained in answer D is incorrect, as it has been taken from the definition of a motor vehicle under the Vehicles (Crime) Act 2001.

Road Traffic, para. 3.1.2.1

Answer 1.2

Answer **C** — Under s. 185(1) of the Road Traffic Act 1988, a motor vehicle is a mechanically propelled vehicle, intended *or* adapted for use on roads. It follows that if a vehicle is not intended or adapted for use on roads, it will not be a motor vehicle for these purposes.

A vehicle is 'intended' for use on the roads, if it was intended that it should be so used *when it was manufactured*. It is immaterial that it is not being used on a road now and answer A is therefore incorrect.

The test will be an objective one — but it does not look at the intention of the owner (*Chief Constable of Avon and Somerset* v *Fleming* [1987] RTR 378). Answer B is therefore incorrect.

Answer D is incorrect because it is immaterial whether the vehicle has been adapted for use on roads, as it was intended to be so used.

Road Traffic, para. 3.1.2.1

Answer 1.3

Answer **A** — Removing an engine from a vehicle does not stop it from being 'mechanically propelled', if you can show that the engine can easily be replaced (*Newberry* v *Simmonds* [1961] 2 All ER 318). Answers C and D are therefore incorrect.

1. Classifications and Concepts

A vehicle that is being towed by another will still be a motor vehicle (*Cobb* v *Whorton* [1971] RTR 392). Answers B and D are therefore incorrect.

Road Traffic, para. 3.1.2.1

Answer 1.4

Answer **B** — A motor-assisted pedal cycle will be a 'mechanically propelled vehicle' even when it is being pedalled (*Floyd* v *Bush* [1953] 1 WLR 242). Answer D is incorrect.

An electrically assisted pedal cycle will *not* qualify as a 'mechanically propelled vehicle', and the only qualification or authority to ride one on the road is that you are 14 years old or over. Answer A is incorrect.

In the case of *Chief Constable of North Yorkshire Police* v *Saddington* [2001] RTR 227, the Divisional Court upheld an earlier decision by magistrates that a petrol-driven micro-scooter *would* qualify as a 'motor vehicle'. For a vehicle to qualify as a 'motor vehicle' it must first be a 'mechanically propelled vehicle', therefore answer C is incorrect.

Road Traffic, para. 3.1.2.1

Answer 1.5

Answer **B** — Statement 1 is incorrect. If a vehicle has been adapted to carry passengers and their effects, as well as goods, it will *not* be a 'passenger vehicle' (*Flower Freight Co. Ltd* v *Hammond* [1963] 1 QB 275).

Statement 2 is a correct statement. A passenger-carrying vehicle, which is constructed to carry more than 8 but no more than 16 passengers, will be classed as a 'mini-bus'. (If the figure is more than 16, the vehicle will be classed as a 'large bus'.)

Consequently, answers A, C and D are incorrect.

Road Traffic, para. 3.1.2.2

Answer 1.6

Answer **D** — Under s. 108(1) of the Road Traffic Act 1988, 'medium-sized' goods vehicles are those constructed to carry or haul goods, which are not adapted to carry more than 9 passengers, *including* the driver.

The maximum permissible weight of such a vehicle will exceed 3.5 tonnes.

Answer D is the only option that covers accurately both points and therefore answers A, B and C are incorrect.

Road Traffic, para. 3.1.2.3

Answer 1.7

Answer **C** — Under s. 108(1) of the Road Traffic Act 1988, the definition of a 'moped' is divided between those that were first used before 1 August 1977, and those first used on or after this date. Early mopeds (i.e. those in the first group) had to have pedals fitted, with an engine size not exceeding 50 cc. There was no restriction on speed. Answer B is therefore incorrect because pedals were not required on mopeds first used after the relevant date.

Mopeds which fall into the newer category are required to have a maximum design speed of 50 kilometres per hour and an engine size not exceeding 50 cc.

Answers A and D are a mixture of the definition of a moped, and the definition of a 'Learner Motor Bicycle' (which must *either* be propelled by electric power *or* have an engine size not exceeding 125 cc) and are therefore incorrect.

Road Traffic, para. 3.1.2.4

Answer 1.8

Answer **A** — The general test which a court will apply is whether an *ordinary person* (not a reasonable person) would say that there had been an accident in all the circumstances. Answer D is therefore incorrect. It is immaterial what the driver of the vehicle thought at the time, and answer C is incorrect.

The term 'accident' *will* include a deliberate act committed by the driver of a vehicle, such as ramming a gate (*Chief Constable of Staffordshire* v *Lees* [1981] RTR 506). Consequently, answer B is incorrect.

Road Traffic, para. 3.1.3.2

Answer 1.9

Answer **B** — It is possible for more than one person to be the 'driver' of a vehicle as s. 192(1) of the Road Traffic Act 1988 makes provision for the 'steersman' to be a 'driver'. This was confirmed in the case of *Tyler* v *Whatmore* [1976] RTR 83, when one person was sitting in the driver's seat and the other leaned across and operated the steering wheel. Answer A is therefore incorrect.

The only situation where the above rule does not apply is in a case of causing death by dangerous driving under s. 1 of the 1988 Act. Answer C is incorrect, as the rule *will* apply in the case of dangerous driving.

Answer D is incorrect because the rule does allow for both to be charged, subject to the exception above.

Road Traffic, para. 3.1.3.3

1. Classifications and Concepts

Answer 1.10

Answer **B** — For the purposes of road traffic offences, a person who takes out a vehicle remains the 'driver' of it until he or she has completed that journey. Therefore, even if the vehicle is stationary for some time, the person may still be the 'driver' if he or she has not completed the journey (see *Jones* v *Prothero* [1952] 1 All ER 434) (answer A is incorrect). Answer D is incorrect as this period could be for some time. The fact that the person had not set the handbrake, or was using the brake, is not relevant in this context, as the offence would still be made out if the handbrake was set. However, this evidence would probably assist in any prosecution. Answer C is therefore incorrect.

Road Traffic, para. 3.1.3.3

Answer 1.11

Answer **C** — The question is designed to test whether a person is **not** driving a vehicle. There are many different cases ruling on whether or not a person is 'driving' a vehicle. This is because the question is one of *fact* and courts are largely left to decide each on its own merits.

The three cases covered by the question offer helpful guidance. In *R* v *MacDonagh* [1974] RTR 372, the defendant was pushing his car, while leaning through the window to steer it. He was held *not* to be 'driving'. The person *was* 'driving' in *Gunnell* v *DPP* [1994] RTR 151, where the person was sitting astride his motorbike and was pushing it along with both feet. In *Jones* v *Pratt* [1983] RTR 54, the person was *not* driving when he was the front seat passenger in a car and grabbed the steering wheel suddenly, to stop the driver hitting an animal.

Contrast *Jones* v *Pratt* with *Tyler* v *Whatmore* in Answer 1.9. The main difference between the two cases would appear to be that in the latter case, Tyler was in control for a little while, whereas in the former, Jones was in control only momentarily. However, as this is a question of fact, there are no guarantees that a court will follow these approaches in every case.

Consequently, answers A, B and D are incorrect.

Road Traffic, para. 3.1.3.4

Answer 1.12

Answer **D** — Acts which are merely preparatory will not amount to attempting to drive. Merely sitting in a car would not be sufficient, as this is still a preparatory act. Answer C is therefore incorrect.

1. Classifications and Concepts

It has been held that, where a defendant sits in the driver's seat of a car and tries to put his or her house keys in the ignition, that behaviour may be enough to prove a charge of 'attempting to drive' (*Kelly* v *Hogan* [1982] RTR 352). Answer A is therefore incorrect.

The fact that the vehicle is incapable of being driven will not prevent a charge involving an 'attempt' to drive (*R* v *Farrance* [1978] RTR 225). Answer B is incorrect because the question asks for the *first* point at which the defendant could be guilty of 'attempting' to drive.

Road Traffic, para. 3.1.3.5

Answer 1.13

Answer **A** — The case of *DPP* v *Watkins* [1989] 2 WLR 966 outlines the principles to be applied when considering whether or not a person is 'in charge' of a vehicle.

Where the defendant is the owner of the vehicle, *or* where he or she has recently driven it, it will be for him or her to show that there was no likelihood of his or her resuming control while he or she was drunk.

Where the defendant is not the owner, or has not recently driven the vehicle, the prosecution will only need to show that the defendant was in voluntary control of the vehicle, or intended to become so in the immediate future. Answers B and D are incorrect for this reason.

Answer C is incorrect, as the defendant must show that it is *unlikely* that he will drive while unfit, not that he had no *intention* of doing so — a slight difference in wording, but nevertheless important in the context of the case.

Road Traffic, para. 3.1.3.6

Answer 1.14

Answer **B** — The 'keeper' of a vehicle can be a different person to the 'owner'. Whereas the 'owner' of the vehicle will remain so until he or she disposes of the vehicle, the 'keeper' can cease to be so if he or she temporarily parts with the vehicle (*R* v *Parking Adjudicator, ex parte The Mayor and Burgesses of the London Borough Council of Wandsworth* [1996] *The Times*, 22 July).

Therefore, while HILTON has not transferred ownership of the vehicle, he is no longer the 'keeper', albeit on a temporary basis. Answers A and D are therefore incorrect.

Section 62(2) of the Vehicle Excise and Registration Act 1994 states that a person

1. Classifications and Concepts

'keeps' the vehicle if he or she causes it to be on a road for any period, however short, when it is not in use there. Therefore, answer C is incorrect.

Road Traffic, para. 3.1.3.7

Answer 1.15

Answer **C** — When a person's movements are beyond his or her control, or his or her actions are involuntary, he or she will not generally be liable in criminal law as the element of *actus reus* is not present. It is also highly likely that because there is no willed action or omission by the defendant, he or she will not have the required state of mind (*mens rea*). A defence is provided in such circumstances, namely 'automatism'. Answers A and D are therefore incorrect.

There is no automatic defence of *automatism*; it will be available only in certain circumstances (answer B is therefore incorrect). If a person has a particular medical condition, which is likely to occur when he or she is driving, he or she has a duty to take reasonable steps to avoid driving when the symptoms are likely to arise (*R v Sibbles* [1959] Crim LR 660). This case is supported by *Moses v Winder* [1981] RTR 37 (which relates specifically to a diabetic undergoing a hypoglycaemic attack).

Road Traffic, para. 3.1.3.8

Answer 1.16

Answer **C** — The vehicle will be 'on a road' in both scenarios. In relation to scenario 1, if a vehicle is partly on the road and partly on some other privately-owned land, it can be treated as being on a 'road' for the purposes of road traffic legislation (*Randall v Motor Insurers' Bureau* [1969] 1 All ER 21).

The answer to scenario 2 is slightly more complicated. The definition of a road, under s. 192(1) of the Road Traffic Act 1988, includes 'any highway'. A 'highway' is a way over which the public has a right to pass and re-pass by foot, horse or vehicle (*Lang v Hindhaugh* [1986] RTR 271). Highways will include 'public bridleways'. Therefore, logically, if a 'bridleway' is a 'highway', and a 'highway' is a 'road', then a 'bridleway' is also a 'road'.

Consequently, answers A, B and D are incorrect.

Road Traffic, paras 3.1.3.9, 3.1.3.11

Answer 1.17

Answer **C** — The situation regarding car parks becoming roads was reviewed as a result of two cases, namely, *Clarke v Kato* and *Cutter v Eagle Star Insurance Co. Ltd* [1998]

1. Classifications and Concepts

1 WLR 1647. Both of these cases were reviewed on appeal in the House of Lords, where the plaintiffs argued that there was no justification in extending the definition of a 'road' under the Road Traffic Act 1988. The car park in each case was provided solely for parking vehicles. Their Lordships held that whether a particular location falls within the definition of a road under the Act will ultimately be one of fact for the courts to decide. Also, that it would only be in exceptional circumstances that a car park could fall within the definition of a road. The court further held that the parking bays within a car park *could not* be regarded as an integral part of the highway, leading into the car park. Consequently, answers A, B and D are incorrect.

Road Traffic, para. 3.1.3.9

Answer 1.18

Answer **A** — In order for a place to be a 'public place', it must be shown by the prosecution that:

- the people admitted to the place are members of the public and are admitted for that reason, and not because they belong to a certain or special class of the public; *and*
- those people are so admitted with the permission, express or implied, of the owner of the land

(*DPP* v *Vivier* [1991] RTR 205).

The above case shows that the place in question must be open to *all* members of the public, without restriction (answer B is therefore incorrect). It is irrelevant whether the people are there with permission if only restricted members of the public are present. The two requirements from the *Vivier* case go hand in hand and answer C is therefore incorrect.

The fact that people had to pay to enter the land is completely irrelevant as to whether it is a public place. It is the *class of people* that are allowed entry (or not) that is important. If the fête had been open to *all* members of the public and they had all been made to pay, it would have been a public place. (Answer D is therefore incorrect.)

Road Traffic, para. 3.1.3.10

Answer 1.19

Answer **A** — The circumstances in the question mirror those in the case of *R* v *DPP, ex parte Taussik* [2001] ACD 10. In this case, the Divisional Court took the view that the

1. Classifications and Concepts

evidence provided by the police was very thin, and that they had not shown that motorists other than residents used the access road regularly. This meant that the court could not find that the road was a public place. The court held that such a road *could* become a public place (therefore answers B and D are incorrect), but it was essential that the prosecution provided *clear* evidence that the road was used by motorists other than residents and that they should present factual details of who used the road and for what purpose. Answer C is incorrect for this reason.

Road Traffic, para. 3.1.3.10

Answer 1.20

Answer **B**—Statement 1 is incorrect. In cases where a dispute arises as to whether a place is a 'public place', it will be for the *prosecution* to show that it is in fact a public place.

Statement 2 is a correct statement. For a place which is ostensibly *public* in its nature to become a *private* place either permanently or temporarily, there needs to be some form of physical obstruction to overcome in order to enter that place (*R v Waters* (1963) 107 SJ 275).

Consequently, answers A, C and D are incorrect.

Road Traffic, para. 3.1.3.10

Answer 1.21

Answer **D** — Offences relating to 'using' a vehicle are generally committed by the driver and the driver's employer. For the employer to commit the offence of 'using', the person driving the vehicle must be doing so in the ordinary course of his or her employer's business (*West Yorkshire Trading Standards Service* v *Lex Vehicle Leasing Ltd* [1996] RTR 70). It must be proved that:

- the employer owned the vehicle;
- the driver was employed by the employer; *and*
- the driver was driving in the ordinary course of his or her employment

(*Jones* v *DPP* [1999] RTR 1).

It is immaterial that the employer has not specifically authorised the employee to use the vehicle in such a way (*Richardson* v *Baker* [1976] RTR 56). Answers A and B are therefore incorrect.

The owner of a trailer who is responsible for putting it on a road will not escape liability by arguing that it was being drawn and therefore 'used' by someone else, (*Forwarding Ltd* v *DPP* [1989] RTR 239).

Answer C is therefore incorrect.

Road Traffic, para. 3.1.3.13

1. Classifications and Concepts

Answer 1.22

Answer **D** — Statement 1 is incorrect. If a vehicle is shown to be a 'motor vehicle' and it is on a road, it may be said to be in 'use', even if it is in such a state that it cannot be driven (*Pumbien* v *Vines* [1996] RTR 37).

Statement 2 is also incorrect. It is generally the case that a passenger in a car does not 'use' the vehicle. However, if a passenger arranges to travel in or on a vehicle for his or her benefit, he or she will 'use' the vehicle (*Cobb* v *Williams* [1973] RTR 113). A passenger can also 'use' a vehicle if there is an element of 'joint enterprise' (*O'Mahoney* v *Jollife and Motor Insurers' Bureau* [1999] RTR 245).

Consequently, answers A, B and C are incorrect.

Road Traffic, para. 3.1.3.13

Answer 1.23

Answer **B** — 'Causing' will involve some degree of dominance or control, or express mandate from the 'causer'.

Causing requires both positive action and knowledge by the defendant, (*Price* v *Cromack* [1975] 1 WLR 988). Therefore it is not enough that the person in charge is aware an offence is being committed; he or she must have done something to contribute to it. Neither person in the scenario could meet these criteria, as neither 'ordered' the offences to be committed (one person was unaware of what was going on).

Further, wilful blindness by employers to their employees' unlawful actions is not enough to amount to 'causing' the offence, (*Redhead Freight Ltd* v *Shulman* (1989) RTR 1). Answers A, C and D are incorrect for these reasons.

Road Traffic, para. 3.1.3.15

Answer 1.24

Answer **D** — Generally in order to prove a case of 'permitting' there must be proof of knowledge by the defendant of the vehicle's use *and* of the unlawful nature of that use. In other words, there must be proof that the defendant knew the vehicle was being used and that the driver was committing an offence by using it. Answers A, B and C are incorrect for this reason.

Road Traffic, para. 3.1.3.16

2 | Offences Involving Standards of Driving

STUDY PREPARATION

Offences involving standards of driving are among the most frequently encountered of road traffic offences. The key to understanding such offences — and any relevant defences — lies in knowing:

- the classification of vehicle covered by the offence;
- the *place* in which the offence can be committed; *and*
- the mental element required.

It should be noted that there is only one standard of driving that is acceptable of any driver, irrespective of his or her particular driving experience or qualifications.

It is also worth noting the application of road traffic law to police drivers and those from other emergency services.

Under the Police Reform Act 2002, police officers and police community support officers (PCSOs) are given additional powers to deal with drivers who use vehicles to cause harassment to members of the public. Finally, the much publicised law relating to the use of hand-held mobile phones was introduced in December 2003, and receives attention in this chapter.

QUESTIONS

Question 2.1

Which statement below most accurately describes where an offence may be committed, and in which type of vehicle, under s. 1 of the Road Traffic Act 1988 (causing death by dangerous driving)?

2. Offences Involving Standards of Driving

A Motor vehicle, on a road only.
B Mechanically propelled vehicle, on a road or public place.
C Motor vehicle, on a road or public place.
D Mechanically propelled vehicle, on a road only.

Question 2.2

HENNIGAN was driving a stolen vehicle and WEBB was a passenger. They were driving at 60 mph, approaching a junction, when HENNIGAN told WEBB to pull the handbrake up. He tried to do a handbrake turn, but lost control when WEBB pulled the handbrake, and collided with a wall. WEBB was killed in the accident, but HENNIGAN survived.

Would HENNIGAN be guilty of causing the death of WEBB by dangerous driving in these circumstances?

A Yes, if it can be shown he was a substantial cause of WEBB's death.
B No, as WEBB contributed substantially to his own death.
C Yes, if it can be shown he was the sole cause of WEBB's death.
D Yes, if it can be shown he contributed in some way to WEBB's death.

Question 2.3

DALEY was driving her car on the approach to a zebra crossing when some children were crossing the road. When DALEY applied her brakes, they failed and she knocked over a child, injuring her. DALEY's car was examined and it was found that her brake discs were worn so much that they did not work. DALEY stated that she had heard the brakes squealing earlier in her journey, but had not realised how bad they were.

What further evidence, if any, would be required in order to convict DALEY of driving dangerously?

A That it would have been obvious to a competent and careful driver that driving the vehicle in that condition would be dangerous.
B No further evidence is required; DALEY may be convicted on these facts alone.
C DALEY could not be convicted of dangerous driving, as she was unaware of the dangerous condition of her car.
D That it should have been obvious to DALEY that driving the vehicle in that condition would be dangerous.

2. Offences Involving Standards of Driving

Question 2.4

NEWMAN was involved in an accident where he drove into the wall of a house, situated on a sharp bend. Nobody was injured in the accident, but substantial damage was caused to the house. There were no witnesses to the accident itself. However, GORDON told the police that NEWMAN had overtaken her before the bend and, in her opinion, he was driving too fast.

What evidence would GORDON be able to give, in order to support a prosecution against NEWMAN for dangerous driving?

A None, as no people suffered injury or death as a direct result of the accident.
B That the vehicle was driven below the standards expected of a competent and careful driver, prior to the accident.
C None, as GORDON was not a witness to the accident itself, her evidence amounts to 'hearsay' evidence.
D That the vehicle was driven far below the standards expected of a competent and careful driver, prior to the accident.

Question 2.5

Which of the following statements, if either, is/are correct in relation to offences under ss. 1 and 2A of the Road Traffic Act 1988 (causing death by dangerous driving and dangerous driving)?
1. If there is sufficient evidence to prove an offence under s. 1, a charge of manslaughter could be considered in appropriate circumstances.
2. A person may be convicted of dangerous driving if the load he or she is carrying on his or her vehicle is considered to be 'dangerous'.

A Statement 1 only.
B Statement 2 only.
C Both statements.
D Neither statement.

Question 2.6

McCRONE was involved in a road traffic accident when he drove into a parked car, having lost concentration momentarily. At the time of the accident, McCRONE was learning to drive in a driving school car and was accompanied by RIDING, his driving instructor.

2. Offences Involving Standards of Driving

In relation to McCRONE's state of mind, what would the prosecution need to prove in order to convict him of driving without due care and attention?

A Either that McCRONE knew, or was aware of the fact that his driving fell far below the required standard.
B The prosecution have nothing to prove in relation to McCRONE's state of mind, there is no statutory defence.
C That McCRONE was aware of the fact that his driving fell below the required standard.
D The prosecution have nothing to prove in relation to McCRONE's state of mind, but he may have a statutory defence due to his inexperience.

Question 2.7

DILKS was driving his car in the open-air car park of a large shopping centre, on a busy Saturday. It was raining heavily and DILKS decided to soak some pedestrians by driving through puddles. The first group he picked on were standing in a bus shelter. DILKS drove past and sprayed water on the shelter window and nobody got wet. The second group was not protected and several people were soaked as a result of his actions.

Has DILKS committed an offence under s. 3 of the Road Traffic Act 1988, by driving without due consideration?

A Yes, but only in relation to the second group of pedestrians.
B No, as no other drivers were affected by his actions.
C Yes, in relation to both groups of pedestrians.
D No, as the incidents did not take place on a road.

Question 2.8

MUNDIE was driving his car along a country road when, as he was approaching a bend, he crossed the central white line dividing the two lanes. As he crossed the line, he nearly collided with another vehicle.

Would the evidence that MUNDIE crossed the white line be conclusive proof alone of driving without due care and attention, contrary to s. 3 of the Road Traffic Act 1988?

A No, MUNDIE would need to have committed at least one other driving error.
B Yes, depending on MUNDIE's explanation of what happened.
C Yes, no further proof would be required to prove the offence.
D No, a single driving error will not amount to an offence under this section.

2. Offences Involving Standards of Driving

Question 2.9

Section 59 of the Police Reform Act 2002 provides a power of entry to premises, in order to seize and remove a motor vehicle which has been used in circumstances that amount to causing harassment.

What restrictions, if any, does the Act place on the type of premises that can be entered by a constable in uniform, in these circumstances?

A There are no restrictions, a constable may enter any place where the vehicle is reasonably thought to be.

B A constable may enter any place where the vehicle is reasonably thought to be, except a private dwelling and land surrounding it.

C A constable may enter any place where the vehicle is reasonably thought to be, except a private dwelling and land adjoining it.

D A constable may enter any place where the vehicle is reasonably thought to be, except a private dwelling.

Question 2.10

PEARCE is a designated community support officer (CSO) working on a housing estate. He has received a number of complaints from residents about HOGAN riding his motor cycle in a park nearby. Last week, PEARCE stopped HOGAN while he was riding his motor cycle and issued him with a warning under s. 59 of the Police Reform Act 2002, as he had narrowly missed colliding with some children playing football. PEARCE has today received a further complaint about HOGAN, who again rode his motor cycle in the park, nearly injuring a child. PEARCE attended HOGAN's home address and saw the motor cycle on the road outside.

Does PEARCE have the power to seize HOGAN's motor cycle, under s. 59(3)(b) of the Police Reform Act 2002, in these circumstances?

A No, a CSO's power is restricted to stopping vehicles.

B Yes, he has the power to seize and remove the vehicle in these circumstances.

C Yes, provided he is accompanied by a police officer in uniform.

D No, as the motor cycle is no longer being used.

Question 2.11

Section 3A of the Road Traffic Act 1988 deals with offences of causing death by careless driving while the offending driver is under the influence of drink or drugs, or is over the prescribed limit.

2. Offences Involving Standards of Driving

Under s. 3A(1)(c), a police officer may make a request for a sample for analysis from the driver suspected of committing such an offence. When may the request be made?

A Within 18 hours of the accident being reported.
B Within 18 hours of the time of death.
C Within 18 hours of a roadside breath test.
D Within 18 hours of the accident.

Question 2.12

Which statement below most accurately describes where an offence may be committed, and in which type of vehicle, under s. 3A(1)(b) of the Road Traffic Act 1988 (causing death by careless driving while over the prescribed limit)?

A Mechanically propelled vehicle, on a road or public place.
B Mechanically propelled vehicle, on a road only.
C Motor vehicle, on a road only.
D Motor vehicle, on a road or public place.

Question 2.13

Section 38(7) of the Road Traffic Act 1988 refers to the use of the Highway Code in court proceedings. In relation to s. 38, which of the following statements, if either, is/are correct?

1. A failure by a person to observe a provision of the Highway Code may only be used in civil proceedings, to establish or negate any liability as to their driving.
2. The braking distances shown in the Highway Code are admissible in proving speeding cases in court.

A Statement 1 only.
B Statement 2 only.
C Both statements.
D Neither statement.

Question 2.14

YOUNG was a passenger in a motor vehicle that was travelling along a busy dual carriageway. At this time, he was supervising GLOVER, a learner driver. YOUNG received a text message on his mobile phone from his wife, telling him he had to pick up his children from school. At this time, it was not practicable to pull over due to the

2. Offences Involving Standards of Driving

nature of the road; therefore, YOUNG sent a text message to his wife saying that he would do so. YOUNG was not using a hands-free device at this time.

Who, if either, would commit an offence because of YOUNG's use of a mobile phone in these circumstances?

A YOUNG for using the phone and GLOVER for permitting its use.
B Only YOUNG commits the offence in these circumstances.
C Neither, as it was not practicable for GLOVER to stop in the circumstances.
D Neither, as YOUNG did not make a telephone call.

Question 2.15

Constable PIERCE was dealing with a road traffic accident, which involved serious injuries to one driver. The driver of the other vehicle left the scene without stopping. A Police National Computer (PNC) check revealed that the registered keeper of the vehicle, LOWE, lived nearby. Constable PIERCE attended LOWE's address immediately to ascertain who was driving the vehicle.

What does s. 172 of the Road Traffic Act 1988 say in relation to Constable PIERCE's ability to ascertain these details?

A A request may be made verbally by Constable PIERCE, and LOWE has 28 days in which to reply.
B A request may only be made by post, and LOWE would have 28 days in which to reply.
C A request may be made verbally by Constable PIERCE, and LOWE must reply immediately.
D Constable PIERCE may not make the request, this power is restricted to people authorised by the Chief Officer of Police.

Question 2.16

YORKE was issued with a provisional Fixed Penalty Notice (FPN) for speeding and was sent a document under s. 172 of the Road Traffic Act 1988, requesting details of the driver. When YORKE replied to the notice, he sent a signed letter to the prosecuting authorities admitting he was the driver. However, he did *not* fill out the document issued under s. 172, and returned the unsigned form with his letter. Later, during a court hearing, YORKE pleaded not guilty, claiming that because he had not signed the document issued under s. 172, he had not made a 'statement' under s. 12 of the Road Traffic Offenders Act 1988, and therefore his admission was not admissible.

2. Offences Involving Standards of Driving

Is YORKE's defence likely to succeed in these circumstances?
A No, if the police can show that YORKE deliberately attempted to avoid prosecution by his actions.
B Yes, because he did not complete the correct form, the police had a duty to re-serve the notice.
C Yes, because the form was not signed, the police had a duty to re-serve the notice.
D No, the police are entitled to require the person providing the information to sign the relevant form.

Question 2.17

O'TOOLE was driving an ambulance to a serious injury road traffic accident. O'TOOLE had activated the siren and flashing lights and was approaching a junction controlled by traffic lights, which were showing red. O'TOOLE slowed down on her approach, but drove through the red light. KEYSE, a pedestrian, stepped off the pavement into the path of the vehicle and was struck by the ambulance, sustaining injuries as a result.

In relation to O'TOOLE's driving, which of the following statements is correct?
A Emergency service crews are entitled to pass through red lights, and O'TOOLE may rely on this exemption to defend her driving.
B O'TOOLE will not be liable for the injuries caused to KEYSE in these circumstances, as she warned the pedestrian of her approach.
C O'TOOLE may be guilty of driving without due care and attention, but may have a defence because of the serious nature of the accident she was attending.
D O'TOOLE will be liable for the injuries caused to KEYSE in these circumstances, even though she warned the pedestrian of her approach.

Question 2.18

MARTIN owed BELL a considerable amount of money. BELL threatened to set fire to MARTIN's car if the money was not paid immediately. MARTIN persuaded his brother to lend him the money and he drove to BELL's house. On his way, MARTIN was stopped by the police, who discovered he was a disqualified driver. MARTIN claimed he was acting under duress, and would not have driven had it not been for the threat made by BELL.

Would MARTIN be entitled to claim a defence of duress in these circumstances?
A No, the defence will apply only where death is threatened.

27

2. Offences Involving Standards of Driving

B No, the defence will apply only where death or serious injury are threatened.
C Yes, the defence will apply where serious damage has been threatened.
D No, the defence will not apply in a case of disqualified driving.

Question 2.19

JOHN and BARBARA were divorced and had a 12-year-old daughter who lived with BARBARA. JOHN was concerned for the welfare of his daughter as BARBARA had been displaying violent tendencies towards her. One evening, he was in the pub when he received a text message from his daughter that BARBARA had threatened to harm her with a knife. JOHN drove to BARBARA's house despite the fact that he had consumed 6 pints of beer. He then drove his daughter to his mother's house, 5 miles away, and attended a local police station to report the incident. The officer receiving the report realised that JOHN had been drinking and requested a sample of breath. JOHN was later found to be over the limit and was charged with driving with excess alcohol.

Would JOHN be able to claim the defence of necessity, because of the circumstances leading to his arrest?

A Yes, because his daughter was at risk of serious harm.
B No, because it was his daughter that was at risk of serious harm and not JOHN himself.
C No, because of the distance JOHN drove after picking up his daughter.
D Yes, because his daughter was at risk of serious harm and the driving was not disproportionate to the harm threatened.

2. Offences Involving Standards of Driving

ANSWERS

Answer 2.1

Answer **B** — The offence of causing death by dangerous driving under s. 1 of the Road Traffic Act 1988 may be committed by a person driving a mechanically propelled vehicle on a road or public place. The Act gives a wide meaning to the types of vehicle that may commit the offence (including dumper trucks, cranes and quad bikes), and the location. Answers A, C and D are therefore incorrect.

Road Traffic, para. 3.2.2

Answer 2.2

Answer **D** — To prove an offence under s. 1 of the Road Traffic Act 1988 (causing death by dangerous driving), it must be shown that a person other than the defendant died. The driving by the defendant must be shown to have been a cause of the death. It is not necessary to show that it was the sole or even a substantial cause of death (*R v Hennigan* [1971] 3 All ER 133). Answers A and C are therefore incorrect.

It is irrelevant whether or not the person killed contributed to the incident, which resulted in his or her death. Answer B is therefore incorrect.

Road Traffic, para. 3.2.2.1

Answer 2.3

Answer **A** — Section 2A(2) of the Road Traffic Act 1988 states:

(2) A person is also to be regarded as driving dangerously for the purposes of sections 1 and 2 above if it would be obvious to a competent and careful driver that driving the vehicle in its current state would be dangerous.

The test is an objective one which looks at the manner of driving and *not* at the defendant's state of mind. It must be proved that:

- the dangerous condition would itself have been obvious to a competent and careful driver; *or*
- the defendant actually *knew* of its condition

2. Offences Involving Standards of Driving

(*R v Strong* [1995] Crim LR 428).

Answer B is incorrect, as the prosecution has to prove one of the above requirements.

Answer C is incorrect for the same reason.

Answer D is incorrect as the dangerous driving must have been obvious to a competent and careful driver — not simply to DALEY herself.

However, see the case of *R v Marchant and Muntz* [2003] Crim LR 806, where the prosecution failed to convince the Court of Appeal that a vehicle was dangerous as a result of its being 'manufactured' in that way.

Road Traffic, paras 3.2.2.2, 3.2.2.3

Answer 2.4

Answer **D** — For the purposes of s. 1 of the Road Traffic Act 1988, under s. 2A(1) of the Act a person is to be regarded as driving dangerously if:

(a) the way he drives falls *far* below what would be expected of a competent and careful driver; *and*
(b) it would be obvious to a competent and careful driver that driving in that way would be dangerous.

(Answer B is incorrect, as the 'far' is missing.)

Answer C is incorrect because evidence showing how a particular vehicle was being driven before the incident itself may be given in support of the charge of dangerous driving. GORDON's 'opinion' would be relevant, because of the wording of s. 2A(1)(b) above.

Under s. 2A(3) of the 1988 Act, 'dangerous' refers to danger either of injury to a person or of serious damage to property. Answer A is therefore incorrect.

Road Traffic, para. 3.2.2.2

Answer 2.5

Answer **C** — Both statements are correct. In relation to statement 1, an offence under s. 1 of the Road Traffic Act 1988 *may* also amount to manslaughter (*R v Governor of Holloway Prison, ex parte Jennings* [1983] 1 AC 624). However, it should be noted that charging a person with manslaughter in these circumstances would be a rare occurrence.

In relation to statement 2, s. 2A(2) of the 1988 Act states that a person will be guilty of dangerous driving if it would be obvious to a competent and careful driver that driving the vehicle in its current state would be dangerous.

2. Offences Involving Standards of Driving

Section 2A(4) of the Act goes on to say that in determining for the purposes of subsection (2) the state of the vehicle, regard may be had to anything attached to or carried on it or in it and to the manner in which it is attached or carried.

Consequently, answers A, B and D are incorrect.

Road Traffic, para. 3.2.2.2

Answer 2.6

Answer **B** — 'Due care and attention' is the standard of driving that would be expected from a reasonable, prudent and competent driver in all the attendant circumstances. Once the prosecution has proved that the defendant has departed from that standard, and that his or her actions were 'voluntary', the offence is complete. There is no requirement to prove any *knowledge* or *awareness* by the defendant that his or her driving fell below that standard (*R* v *Lawrence* [1981] RTR 217). Answers A and C are therefore incorrect. There is only one *objective* standard of driving, which is expected of *all* drivers — even learner drivers (*McCrone* v *Riding* [1938] 1 All ER 157). Answer D is therefore incorrect.

Road Traffic, para. 3.2.4

Answer 2.7

Answer **A** — An offence is committed under s. 3 of the Road Traffic Act 1988 when a person drives a mechanically propelled vehicle on a road or public place, without due care and attention, or without due consideration for other persons using the road or *place*. As the offence may be committed in a public place, answer D is incorrect.

Other persons using the road/public place can include pedestrians who are deliberately sprayed with water from a puddle or passengers in a vehicle (*Pawley* v *Wharldall* [1965] 2 All ER 757. Answer B is therefore incorrect.

It must be shown that some other person was inconvenienced by the defendant's actions (*Dilks* v *Bowman-Shaw* [1981] RTR 4). No people were affected in the first group, answer C is therefore incorrect.

Road Traffic, para. 3.2.4.1

Answer 2.8

Answer **B** — Breaching certain road traffic regulations will not always provide conclusive proof of an offence of driving without due care and attention, pursuant

2. Offences Involving Standards of Driving

to s. 3 of the Road Traffic Act 1988. *However*, crossing a central white line without explanation *has* been held as conclusive proof of the offence, (see *Mundi* v *Warwickshire Police* [2001] EWHC Admin 448). Consequently, answers A, C and D are incorrect.

Road Traffic, para. 3.2.4.1

Answer 2.9

Answer **D** — Section 59(3)(c) of the Police Reform Act 2002 provides a power of entry to premises, in order to seize and remove a motor vehicle which has been used in circumstances that amount to causing harassment, if necessary by force (s. 59(3)(d)). The description of the power contained in s. 59(7) of the Act excludes entry into a 'private dwelling house' (therefore answer A is incorrect). However, s. 59(7) *does not* exclude entry into other areas surrounding or adjoining a dwelling, such as driveways, garages, outhouses or other land. Answers B and C are incorrect for this reason.

Road Traffic, para. 3.2.4.2

Answer 2.10

Answer **B** — To exercise one of the powers under s. 59(3) of the Act, a constable in uniform must have reasonable grounds for believing that a motor vehicle is being used on any occasion in a manner which contravenes s. 3 or s. 34 of the Road Traffic Act 1988, (careless/inconsiderate driving and prohibition of off-road driving), and is causing/likely to cause alarm, distress or annoyance to members of the public, (s. 59(1)). Under s. 59(2) of the Act, a constable may also exercise a power under s. 59(3) if he/she has reasonable grounds for believing a motor vehicle *has been* used in circumstances outlined above. Answer D is incorrect.

The powers listed under s. 59(3) enable a constable in uniform to stop motor vehicles in contravention of s. 59(1) or (2) above, to seize and remove motor vehicles, enter any premises (except a dwelling) and use reasonable force if necessary. A vehicle may only be seized if a warning has previously been issued to the user of the vehicle that it will be seized if the use continues or is repeated and it appears to the officer that the use *has* continued or been repeated after the warning. The power to stop, seize and remove vehicles can be conferred on a CSO, but he or she may not enter premises unless accompanied and supervised by a constable in uniform. Answers A and C are therefore incorrect.

Road Traffic, para. 3.2.4.2

2. Offences Involving Standards of Driving

Answer 2.11

Answer **D** — Under s. 3A(1)(c) of the Road Traffic Act 1988, a police officer may request a sample from the driver who has committed an offence under s. 3A(1), within 18 hours of the *driving which caused the death*, and not after the death itself, or the reporting of the accident, or the requesting of any other samples. Answers A, B and C are therefore incorrect. This will presumably present practical problems where the injured person dies *after* the 18 hours elapses.

Road Traffic, para. 3.2.7

Answer 2.12

Answer **D** — Three separate offences may be committed under s. 3A(1) of the Road Traffic Act 1988, which deals with causing the death of a person while driving without due care and attention or without reasonable consideration. *All three* may be committed on a road *or* public place, and answers B and C are incorrect. The type of vehicle depends on which subsection the person is charged under:

- s. 3A(1)(a) — *unfit through drink or drugs* — *mechanically propelled vehicle;*
- s. 3A(1)(b) — *exceeding the prescribed limit* — *motor vehicle only;* and
- s. 3A(1)(c) — *failing to provide a specimen for analysis* — *motor vehicle only.*

The question deals with an offence under s. 3A(1)(b), (*exceeding the prescribed limit*), which may only be committed in a *motor vehicle*, which means that answers A and B are incorrect.

There seems no obvious reason for the legislation to have been written in this way, other than the fact that the offences under s. 3A mirror those under ss. 4 and 5 of the Act (offences committed by the driver of a *mechanically propelled vehicle* and a *motor vehicle* respectively).

Road Traffic, para. 3.2.7

Answer 2.13

Answer **D** — Statement 1 is incorrect. Under s. 38(7) of the Road Traffic Act 1988, a failure by a person to observe a provision of the Highway Code may be used in civil proceedings *or* criminal cases to establish or negate any liability as to their driving.

2. Offences Involving Standards of Driving

Statement 2 is also incorrect; the braking distances shown in the Highway Code are *not* admissible in proving speeding cases in court, as they amount to *hearsay* (R v Chadwick [1975] Crim LR 105).

Consequently, answers A, B and C are incorrect.

Road Traffic, para. 3.2.8

Answer 2.14

Answer **B** — There are three specific offences which may be prosecuted under s. 42 of the Road Traffic Act 1988:

- driving a motor vehicle while using a hand-held mobile telephone;
- permitting another person to *drive* a motor vehicle while using a hand-held mobile telephone; *and*
- using a hand-held mobile telephone while supervising a learner driver.

The offence of permitting the use of such a device will normally be directed at employers who require or expect drivers to make or receive communications using a hand-held device when driving. Since YOUNG was not driving the vehicle, GLOVER will not be guilty of this offence and answer A is incorrect.

The offence will be committed under *any* of the above three subsections if the hand-held device is used either to make a telephone call *or* to *perform any other interactive communication function by transmitting and receiving data*, which will include sending a text message, fax, e-mail or picture. Answer D is therefore incorrect.

Lastly, there is a specific defence to this offence, if the driver (or supervisor) can show that he or she was using the hand-held device to make an emergency call to the police, fire, ambulance or other emergency services, that he or she was acting in response to a genuine emergency *and* that it was impracticable to cease driving (or for the provisional licence holder to cease driving). All three of these circumstances must apply before the defence can be considered. Since YOUNG's telephone call was not an emergency, it is immaterial that it was not practicable to stop, and he would have no defence. Answer C is therefore incorrect.

Road Traffic, para. 3.2.8.1

Answer 2.15

Answer **C** — Under s. 172(2) of the Road Traffic Act 1988, where the driver of a vehicle has committed an offence to which the section applies (this includes ss. 3 and 170

2. Offences Involving Standards of Driving

(accidents)), the keeper of the vehicle shall give information as to the identity of the driver as required by or on behalf of a chief officer of police.

There is no mention of a person having to be authorised to make such a request on behalf of the chief officer and therefore it can be assumed that as Constable PIERCE is acting in the course of his duties, he is acting on behalf of the chief officer. Answer D is therefore incorrect.

When a request is made by post, the keeper has 28 days in which to reply. The 1988 Act does not state that *all* requests must be made by post and answer B is therefore incorrect. On the contrary, the case of *Lowe* v *Lester* [1987] RTR 30 indicates that requests may be made verbally, and the information must be provided within a reasonable time, which may in the prevailing circumstances mean *immediately*. Therefore, answer A is incorrect.

Road Traffic, para. 3.2.9

Answer 2.16

Answer **D** — When a person is issued with a notice under s. 172 of the Road Traffic Act 1988, in order to meet the requirements of s. 12 of the Road Traffic Offenders Act 1988 and face proceedings, he or she is required to sign the notice giving details of the driver of the vehicle at that time. The circumstances in the question were examined in a number of court cases. In *Jones* v *DPP* [2004] EWHC 236, the defendant provided written information to the prosecuting authorities, as opposed to completing the relevant form. The court held that it is enough that the person gives the relevant information in writing, and the defendant's conviction was upheld. Answer B is therefore incorrect.

In *Mawdesly and Yorke* v *Chief Constable of Cheshire Constabulary* [2004] 1 All ER 58, it was claimed that the defendant had provided the relevant information but had omitted to sign the notice served under s. 172. The court held that the conviction should be set aside. However, this evidential loophole was closed when the Divisional Court ruled that a chief officer is entitled to *require* the person providing the information to sign the relevant notice served under s. 172 (*Francis* v *DPP* [2004] EWHC Admin 591). Answer C is incorrect — there is no requirement for the police to re-serve the notice if either of the above circumstances occur; neither do the police have to prove that the person deliberately attempted to avoid prosecution so answer A is incorrect.

Road Traffic, para. 3.2.9

2. Offences Involving Standards of Driving

Answer 2.17

Answer **B** — There is no special exemption for emergency drivers with regard to standards of driving (*R* v *O'Toole* (1971) 55 Cr App R 206), and they will be judged against the standards of care which apply to *all* drivers. There is an exemption which allows emergency drivers to pass through red lights under the Traffic Signs Regulations 2002 (SI 2002 No. 3113), reg. 36(1)(b). However, this *does not* exempt emergency drivers from having to drive with due care and attention. Answer A is therefore incorrect.

Answer C is incorrect because of the case of *DPP* v *Harris* [1995] RTR 100, where the driver of a police surveillance vehicle following a suspect drove through a red light. The court held that even though the suspects were being followed to the scene of an armed robbery, the seriousness of the circumstances did not provide an exemption.

Answer D is incorrect (and consequently answer B is correct), because of the ruling in the case of *Keyse* v *Commissioner of the Metropolitan Police* [2001] EWHC Cir. 715. This was a case defended on behalf of a police driver, but would presumably apply to other emergency service drivers. The court held that the police driver, who was driving with the vehicle's visual and audible warning equipment in operation, was not liable for the injuries to a pedestrian who stepped off the pavement into the path of the vehicle.

Road Traffic, para. 3.2.10

Answer 2.18

Answer **B** — The defence(s) of *duress* and *necessity* will apply to cases of dangerous driving, careless and inconsiderate driving *and* driving while disqualified (*R* v *Martin* [1989] RTR 63 and *R* v *Backshall* [1998] 1 WLR 1506). Answer D is therefore incorrect. The defence of duress will only apply where the defendant was forced to commit an offence to avoid death or serious injury (*R* v *Conway* [1989] RTR 35). The defence *will not* apply in cases of criminal damage or where criminal damage has been threatened, no matter how serious. Answers A and C are therefore incorrect.

Road Traffic, para. 3.2.11

Answer 2.19

Answer **C** — A person may claim the defence of 'necessity' when charged with a drink driving offence. The situation was considered in the cases of *DPP* v *Tomkinson* [2001]

2. Offences Involving Standards of Driving

RTR 38 and *DPP* v *Hicks* [2002] EWHC 1638. In *Hicks*, the court found that the defence would be available only if:

- the driving was undertaken to avoid consequences that could not otherwise have been avoided;
- those consequences were inevitable and involved a risk of serious harm to the driver *or someone else for whom he or she was responsible*;
- the driver did no more than reasonably necessary to avoid harm; *and*
- the danger of so driving was not disproportionate to the harm threatened.

This ruling followed the earlier *Tomkinson* case, when the Divisional Court found that the defendant had driven a far greater distance than was necessary to avoid the relevant danger and that the defence would not be available. In the case examined in the question, unquestionably the daughter had been threatened with serious harm. The harm threatened must be serious, not just immediate and unlawful, therefore answer A is incorrect. The defence *may* be used where a person other than the driver is threatened, therefore answer B is incorrect. However, it could be argued that the distance JOHN travelled after picking up his daughter was greater than necessary and that he could have stopped at some point to call the police, which is why answer C is correct and answer D is incorrect.

Road Traffic, para. 3.2.11

3 | Notices of Intended Prosecution

Please note that the questions in this chapter relate to material in the Blackstone's Police Manuals which has been excluded from the OSPRE® Inspectors' Exam syllabus for 2005.

> **STUDY PREPARATION**
>
> Like much road traffic legislation, the law governing notices of intended prosecution (NIPs) is concerned with procedural detail. Once you know which offences are generally covered by the NIP procedure, you then need to learn the procedure required for proper service to be accepted by the courts and any exceptions provided for.
>
> Understanding the purpose behind NIPs will help you in learning all this important procedural detail.

QUESTIONS

Question 3.1

Constable DALTON was following a car being driven by a person whom he recognised as being GIBSON. GIBSON failed to stop for the officer and, following a pursuit, Constable DALTON lost sight of the car. The officer knew GIBSON's home address and attended there straight away, in order to report him for driving without due care and attention. There was no reply at the house. Constable DALTON eventually caught up with GIBSON two days later.

What action should the officer now take, to comply with s. 1 of the Road Traffic Offenders Act 1988 (notice of intended prosecution (NIP))?

A   Issue a verbal NIP personally to GIBSON there and then.
B   Send a written NIP or summons to GIBSON within 12 days.

3. Notices of Intended Prosecution

C Send both a written NIP and summons to GIBSON within 14 days.
D Send a written NIP or summons to GIBSON within 14 days.

Question 3.2

Where a person has been given a verbal warning at the time of an offence, of a notice of intended prosecution (NIP), what proof is required that he or she understood the notice?

A It is for the prosecution to prove that the defendant understood the notice on every occasion.
B If the defendant claims he or she did not understand a verbal notice, it is for the defence to prove this fact.
C It is for the prosecution to prove that the defendant understood the notice, if a written notice was not given at a later date.
D It is for the prosecution to prove that the defendant understood the notice, if the defendant disputes this fact.

Question 3.3

When an offence is committed partly within the jurisdiction of two different courts, which court must hear the case?

A It must be heard in the court where the first offence took place.
B It may be heard in either court area.
C It must be heard in the court where the more serious offence took place.
D It must be heard in the court where the second offence took place.

Question 3.4

HAWKLEY was responsible for failing to stop after an accident in a supermarket car park, when he damaged another car and drove off. A witness took his registration number and reported the accident to Constable DAVIES. The officer sent a notice of intended prosecution (NIP), to HAWKLEY's address as shown on Police National Computer (PNC). However, HAWKLEY had moved. HAWKLEY was traced two months later and, when interviewed, stated he had never received the NIP.

What effect would the failure to serve the NIP have on any future prosecution against HAWKLEY?

A None, as HAWKLEY was at fault for the failure of the service.
B The NIP was not served in time and therefore the case cannot proceed.

3. Notices of Intended Prosecution

C None, a NIP was not required as the offence occurred at the time of an accident.
D None, a NIP was not required as the accident did not occur on a road.

Question 3.5

LEWINSKI was driving his motor vehicle along a main road, approaching a set of traffic lights at a junction. Due to a lack of concentration, LEWINSKI drove through a red light and collided with a heavy goods vehicle. LEWINSKI suffered severe head injuries as a result of the accident and was taken to hospital, where he remained for several weeks. Because of his injuries, LEWINSKI was not able to recall being involved in the accident. The officer in the case is contemplating whether or not a notice of intended prosecution (NIP) should be served on LEWINSKI, for driving through the red light.

Would the officer be correct in serving a NIP because of the serious injuries, in these circumstances?

A Yes, as LEWINSKI was severely injured as a result of the accident.
B No, a NIP is never required when the driver has been involved in an accident.
C It is immaterial whether he was injured or not, because the accident was not of a minor nature.
D Yes, a NIP is always required when the driver is injured as a result of an accident.

Question 3.6

In which of the following scenarios will a notice of intended prosecution (NIP) have been correctly served under s. 1 of the Road Traffic Offenders Act 1988?
1. A NIP was served personally by the officer in the case on the defendant's common law husband.
2. The defendant was on holiday for six weeks. The officer in the case was aware of this but still served a written NIP to the defendant's home address, while the defendant was away.
3. An officer gave a verbal NIP to a motorist, who later claimed that the officer had not specified what offence he was being prosecuted for and was only told that he had committed a 'speeding offence'.

A Scenarios 2 and 3 only.
B All three scenarios.
C Scenarios 1 and 3 only.
D Scenarios 1 and 2 only.

3. Notices of Intended Prosecution

ANSWERS

Answer 3.1

Answer **B** — Under s. 1 of the Road Traffic Offenders Act 1988, before certain offences can be prosecuted, the defendant must have *either* been warned of the possibility of prosecution at the time of the offence, *or* served with a summons (or charged) within 14 days of the offence *or* a notice of intended prosecution (NIP) must have been sent to the registered keeper within 14 days of the offence.

Answer A is incorrect as a verbal NIP may only be given at the time of the offence. If this is not possible, the prosecution is able to send a written one to the keeper's last known address.

Answer C is incorrect as there is no requirement to send both the summons and the written NIP within 14 days; one will suffice. Answer C is also incorrect, as is answer D, because two days have already elapsed since the incident, and the written NIP (or summons) must be sent within 14 days of the *offence committed*.

Road Traffic, para. 3.3.1

Answer 3.2

Answer **A** — If a verbal warning is given at the time of the offence, it must be shown that the defendant understood it (*Gibson* v *Dalton* [1980] RTR 410). Proof that the defendant understood the warning will lie with the *prosecution*. Answer B is incorrect. The prosecution must show this on *every* occasion, whether or not the defendant claims he or she did not understand, or whether a written notice was given at a later date. Answers C and D are therefore incorrect.

Road Traffic, para. 3.3.1

Answer 3.3

Answer **B** — When an offence is committed partly within the jurisdiction of two different courts, it may be heard in *either* court (*Kennet DC* v *Young* [1999] RTR 235). Answers A, C and D are therefore incorrect.

Road Traffic, para. 3.3.1

3. Notices of Intended Prosecution

Answer 3.4

Answer **A** — Section 2(1) of the Road Traffic Offenders Act 1988 states that a notice of intended prosecution (NIP) does not need to be served if at the time or immediately afterwards and owing to the presence of the motor vehicle concerned *on a road* an accident occurred. This means that where an accident occurs on a road, a NIP is not required for a due care offence; however, where an accident occurs in a public place a NIP *will be* required. Answers C and D are therefore incorrect.

A notice must be served on the defendant within 14 days of the offence, if it was not given verbally at the time. However, under s. 2(3) of the 1988 Act, if the defendant contributes to the failure to serve the NIP, then that will not be a bar to his or her conviction. Answer B is therefore incorrect.

Road Traffic, para. 3.3.3

Answer 3.5

Answer **C** — Generally, a notice of intended prosecution (NIP) is *not* required if at the time of the offence, or immediately afterwards, an accident occurred owing to the presence of a motor vehicle on a road (s. 2(1) of the Road Traffic Offenders Act 1988). However, there is an exception to this rule. Where the driver of a motor vehicle is unaware that an accident has taken place because it is so *minor*, there *will* be a need to serve a NIP (*Bentley* v *Dickinson* [1983] RTR 356). Answer B is incorrect, as the exception shows that sometimes an NIP may be required following an accident.

When the accident is so severe that the driver of the vehicle is unable to recall it, a NIP is *not* required (*DPP* v *Pidhajeckyi* [1991] RTR 136). Answer A is incorrect because of the ruling in this case. Answer D is incorrect, as there is nothing in the Act stating that a NIP is required every time a driver is injured in an accident.

Answer C is *correct* because it is *not* relevant whether the driver was injured, as the accident was not of a minor nature (and *Bentley* does not apply), and therefore it falls within the scope of s. 2(1) (above).

Road Traffic, para. 3.3.3

Answer 3.6

Answer **B** — All three of the scenarios are based on decided cases, where the court agreed that the provisions of s. 1(1) of the Road Traffic Act 1988 had been complied with.

Scenario 1 is based on the case of *Hosier* v *Goodall* [1962] 1 All ER 30, where it was decided that a notice served on the defendant's spouse or partner was sufficient.

Scenario 2 is based on the case of *Phipps* v *McCormick* [1972] Crim LR 540, where it was held that if the defendant is not at his or her home address, for instance because he or she is in hospital or on holiday, service to his or her last known address will suffice, even if the police are aware of that fact.

Scenario 3 comes from the case of *Pope* v *Clarke* [1953] 2 All ER 704, where it was held that a purpose of the notice is to alert the defendant of the likelihood of prosecution. It is not necessary to specify which offence is being considered; it is enough that the defendant is made aware of the *nature* of the offence.

Consequently, answers A, C and D are incorrect.

Road Traffic, para. 3.3.5

4 Accidents and Collisions

> **STUDY PREPARATION**
>
> The law relating to road traffic 'accidents' is primarily concerned with obligations on the drivers involved and the offences for failing to comply with those obligations. Throughout this chapter we will use the term 'road traffic collision', which is in line with current policing practice.
>
> The most important bit of this subject is knowing what amounts to an 'accident' or 'collision'. You need to be able to recognise from the fact pattern of a question whether an 'accident' has happened. Then you need to know what obligations the law imposes and upon whom. You also need to know any offences which may apply, along with the attendant police powers.

QUESTIONS

Question 4.1

BENNETT was involved in a road traffic collision, while driving his employer's van. He drove into the rear of a car at a set of traffic lights. BENNETT was asked by the driver of the other vehicle for his name and address only. BENNETT gave his own name, but gave his employer's address as he was driving a works vehicle.

Has BENNETT complied with s. 170(2) of the Road Traffic Act 1988 (duty to stop and give details) in these circumstances?

A No, he should also have given the name of the owner of the vehicle to the other driver.

B No, he should also have given the name of the owner of the vehicle, and the registration number to the other driver.

4. Accidents and Collisions

C Yes, he has complied fully with the requirements of the Act in these circumstances.
D No, he should have given his own address to the other driver, not his employer's.

Question 4.2

CAWTHORN was driving his car and towing a trailer, when he stopped at a shop on the brow of a hill. While he was inside the shop, the coupling which fixed the trailer to the car broke. The trailer rolled down the hill and collided with a parked car causing damage to it.

What obligation does CAWTHORN have to exchange details with the driver of the parked vehicle in these circumstances?

A None, as he was not to blame for the accident.
B He has an obligation to stop and exchange details with the owner.
C None, as he was not driving a vehicle at the time of the accident.
D None, as the trailer is not a mechanically propelled vehicle.

Question 4.3

CUTTER was involved in a collision in a multi-storey car park, which was open to the public at the time. CUTTER was driving out of a parking space in his van when he scraped the side of a parked car. CUTTER failed to stop after the accident; however, a witness noted his registration number. When he was traced by the police, CUTTER stated that he hadn't stopped as he was unaware of the collision.

Who would have responsibility for proving or disproving that CUTTER was unaware of the collision?

A The defence must show on the balance of probabilities he was unaware of the collision.
B The prosecution must show beyond reasonable doubt he would have been aware of the collision.
C The defence must show beyond reasonable doubt he was unaware of the collision.
D The question is not relevant; there was no requirement to stop after the collision as it did not occur on a road.

4. Accidents and Collisions

QUESTION 4.4

HALLINAN was driving a double-decker bus in heavy traffic, when he had to brake sharply to avoid running into the rear of a vehicle travelling in front of him. As a result of the bus braking, PARKER, a passenger on the bus, fell over and injured her head. Another passenger on the bus told HALLINAN of PARKER's injury; however, he carried on driving to the next bus stop a mile away, where he contacted his depot to ask for instructions.

   Would HALLINAN be guilty of failing to stop at the scene of an accident, in these circumstances?

   A No, the bus was the scene of the accident, therefore he was not required to stop immediately.
   B No, as the bus was the only vehicle involved, there was no scene to the accident.
   C Yes, he should have stopped where the injury occurred, which was the scene of the accident.
   D No, as the bus was the only vehicle involved, the accident was not reportable.

Question 4.5

Constable ANGEL was investigating a road traffic collision, during which a pedestrian was injured while crossing the road. The driver of the offending vehicle, ROPER, failed to stop at the scene; however, a witness noted the registration number of his vehicle. Constable ANGEL immediately attended ROPER's home address and the vehicle was parked outside.

   What powers are available to Constable ANGEL, to deal with ROPER in these circumstances?

   A Power of arrest and power of entry, but only if she suspects he has been drinking.
   B Report ROPER for failing to stop; no power of arrest or entry.
   C Power of arrest for failing to stop, but no power of entry.
   D Power of arrest and power of entry if necessary, in these circumstances alone.

Question 4.6

BATES was driving in the early hours of the morning, in a built up area, when he collided with a parked car while negotiating a bend. Damage was caused to the parked car. BATES stopped his car, but as it was so late, there was nobody about.

What must BATES now do, in relation to the damaged car?
A Remain at the scene until someone arrives to give details to.
B Report the collision to the police within 24 hours.
C Make enquiries of his own to find the owner before he leaves.
D Report the accident to the police as soon as practicable.

Question 4.7

While driving his car, DAWSON was involved in a road traffic collision with a motor cycle being ridden by WINTER. WINTER suffered cuts and grazes as a result. The drivers exchanged details and WINTER asked DAWSON for his insurance certificate. DAWSON did not have it with him, but gave WINTER the name of his insurance company and promised to show him the certificate the next day.

Has DAWSON complied with the requirements of s. 170 of the Road Traffic Act 1988 in these circumstances?

A Yes, he is not obliged to produce his insurance certificate to another driver, provided he gives the name of his insurance company.
B No, he must report the collision to the police as soon as reasonably practicable, and produce his insurance certificate within seven days.
C No, he must report the collision to the police as soon as reasonably practicable, and produce his insurance certificate at the same time.
D Yes, provided he produces his insurance certificate to WINTER within 24 hours.

4. Accidents and Collisions

ANSWERS

Answer 4.1

Answer **C** — Under s. 170(2) of the Road Traffic Act 1988, the driver of a vehicle involved in a road traffic collision must stop and *if required to do so* by some person having reasonable grounds, give his or her name and address and also the name and address of the owner of the vehicle, and the registration mark of the vehicle.

Because the driver of the other vehicle did not ask for the name of the owner and the registration mark, Bennett commits no offence by failing to give them. Answers A and B are therefore incorrect.

It has been held that, as the reason for the requirement to 'exchange details' is to allow future communications between parties, the address of the driver's solicitor would satisfy the requirements of s. 170(2) (*DPP* v *McCarthy* [1999] RTR 323). Answer D is therefore incorrect.

Road Traffic, para. 3.4.2

Answer 4.2

Answer **B** — It has been held that even though a driver may not have been to blame for a collision, he or she will still attract the duties imposed by s. 170 of the Road Traffic Act 1988 (*Harding* v *Price* [1948] 1 All ER 283). Answer A is therefore incorrect.

If there has been a break from driving, and a collision occurs while the driver is away from the vehicle, he or she will still be required to fulfil the obligations of s. 170 (*Cawthorn* v *DPP* [2000] RTR 45). In this case, even though the driver was not directly responsible for the accident (the passenger had let off the handbrake), there was still a requirement to comply with s. 170. Answer C is incorrect as there is no requirement for a person to be driving at the time of the accident.

Answer D is incorrect as s. 170(1) requires the driver to stop and exchange details when damage was caused to another vehicle by his or her own vehicle, or a trailer being drawn by it.

Road Traffic, para. 3.4.2

Answer 4.3

Answer **A** — the case of *Cutter* v *Eagle Star Insurance Co. Ltd* [1998] 4 All ER 417 changed the requirements under s. 170 of the Road Traffic Act 1988. Prior to this case,

4. Accidents and Collisions

a collision was not 'reportable' unless it occurred on a road. The section has now been extended to include 'public places'. Since the car park was open to any member of the public, it was a public place and covered by s. 170. Answer D is therefore incorrect.

When a driver alleges he or she was unaware that a collision had taken place, it is for the defence to show *on the balance of probabilities* that this was the case (*Selby* v *Chief Constable of Avon and Somerset* [1988] RTR 216. Answers B and C are therefore incorrect.

Road Traffic, para. 3.4.2

Answer 4.4

Answer **C** — Where injury is caused to a person other than the driver of the vehicle (even if the person was in the vehicle with the offending driver), the driver is required under s.170 of the Road Traffic Act 1988 to stop the vehicle *at the scene*. Answers B and D are incorrect, as the driver in the scenario *was* involved in a reportable accident and was required to stop the bus.

The facts in the question are similar to those in *Hallinan* v *DPP* [1998] Crim LR 754, where the Divisional Court held that the driver of the bus had a duty to stop *at the place and time that the passenger was injured*. The driver was not entitled to claim that the bus itself was the scene of the accident, and by not stopping immediately he was guilty of an offence under s. 170(4). Answer A is therefore incorrect.

Road Traffic, para. 3.4.2

Answer 4.5

Answer **D** — A driver who fails to stop after a road traffic collision commits an offence under s. 170 of the Road Traffic Act 1988. Under s. 71 of the Criminal Justice and Police Act 2001, the offence of failing to stop following a *personal injury* road traffic collision is now an arrestable offence. Answer B is incorrect.

As the offence is now an arrestable offence, it follows that there is a power of entry under the Police and Criminal Evidence Act 1984, if need be by force (and answer C is incorrect). It is immaterial whether or not the officer suspects that the driver has been drinking, because of s. 71 above (although there is a separate power under s. 6(6) of the Road Traffic Act 1988, to enter premises to require a person to provide a specimen of breath, following an injury road traffic collision — see Chapter 5). Answer A is incorrect.

Road Traffic, para. 3.4.3

4. Accidents and Collisions

Answer 4.6

Answer **D** — Under s. 170(2) of the Road Traffic Act 1988 a driver is required to stop safely at the scene and remain there for long enough to allow anyone having a right or reason for doing so to ask for information from the driver (*Lee* v *Knapp* [1967] 2 QB 442). It does not require the driver to make his or her own enquiries to find such a person (*Mutton* v *Bates* [1984] RTR 256). Answer C is therefore incorrect.

The driver is also under a duty to stay with his or her vehicle for a reasonable time for the above requirements (*Ward* v *Rawson* [1978] RTR 498). Answer A is incorrect as there is no requirement to wait until someone happens to arrive.

If a driver does not give details at the scene for whatever reason, he or she is required to report the collision to a police officer or at a police station. This must be done *as soon as reasonably practicable* (and it will be for the court to decide what is reasonable), and in any case within 24 hours.

This *does not* give the driver 24 hours to report the collision — and in most circumstances there is no reason for a collision not to be reported straightaway because of the availability of police officers 24 hours a day. Answer B is therefore incorrect.

Road Traffic, para. 3.4.2.1

Answer 4.7

Answer **C** — If a driver is involved in a collision where injury is caused to another person, he or she must, at the time of the collision, produce a certificate of insurance to a constable *or* any person having reasonable grounds for requiring it (s. 170(5) of the Road Traffic Act 1988). Answer A is therefore incorrect.

If the driver does not produce his or her insurance certificate as required above, he or she *must* report the accident to the police *and* produce an insurance certificate as soon as practicable, and in any case within 24 hours (s. 170(6)).

Answer D is incorrect as once a driver fails to produce a certificate at the scene to the other driver, the requirement moves to reporting the collision and producing the certificate to the police.

Answer B is incorrect as the requirement is to report the collision *and* produce the insurance certificate as soon as practicable and within 24 hours. Under s. 170(7) of the 1988 Act, a person will escape prosecution for failing to produce insurance at the time of the collision, or later at the police station, if he or she produces it within seven days from the collision (usually as a result of the issue of an HO/RT/1). Therefore, although answer B may appear correct, the *first* process must be to report the collision and produce the certificate as soon as practicable.

Road Traffic, para. 3.4.2.3

5 | Drink Driving

> **STUDY PREPARATION**
>
> This is a big one. The areas of law and procedure covered in this chapter are extensive. You will need to know the elements of each of the main drink driving offences first. Entwined with those offences is a range of police powers such as the powers to require breath samples. Recent changes to the Road Traffic Act 1988 allow police officers to administer three preliminary tests — a breath test, a test indicating whether a person is unfit to drive due to drink or drugs, and a test to detect the presence of drugs in a person's body. Failure or refusal to comply with such requirements can lead to further offences and further powers.
>
> It is sometimes helpful to divide this subject area into roadside, police station and hospital procedures.
>
> The evidential issues are also important and there is a great deal of established case law to clarify this area of the legislation.

QUESTIONS

Question 5.1

Constable PITROLA was stopped by GRANGER, who had seen a man in a pub earlier, drinking heavily. The man was now sitting in a car outside the pub and GRANGER feared he might drive. As Constable PITROLA approached the car he saw HART sitting in the driver's seat. HART saw the officer and locked all the doors, refusing to open them again.

> Would Constable PITROLA have a power to enter the vehicle by force to deal with HART under s. 4 of the Road Traffic Act 1988 (in charge of or unfit drive a vehicle)?

5. Drink Driving

A No, GRANGER's suspicion that HART is drunk is not sufficient to provide reasonable suspicion to enter the vehicle.
B Yes, in order to breathalise HART, on reasonable suspicion that he is unfit drive through drink.
C Yes, in order to arrest HART, on reasonable suspicion that he is unfit drive through drink.
D No, as the power provided under this section is to enter a premises and not a vehicle.

Question 5.2

SHELLEY was charged with an offence of being in charge of his motor vehicle on a road, while over the prescribed limit, having been found asleep at the wheel of the vehicle one night. At his court hearing, SHELLEY claimed that he would not have driven the vehicle while he was still unfit to do so.

Who is responsible for proving or disproving SHELLEY's claim, that he was unlikely to drive the vehicle whilst unfit to do so?

A SHELLEY must demonstrate an arguable case that there was no likelihood of him driving whilst unfit to do so.
B The prosecution must demonstrate beyond reasonable doubt that there was a likelihood of SHELLEY driving whilst unfit to do so.
C SHELLEY must demonstrate on the balance of probabilities that there was no likelihood of him driving whilst unfit to do so.
D The prosecution must demonstrate on the balance of probabilities that there was a likelihood of SHELLEY driving whilst unfit to do so.

Question 5.3

Constable McDONALD arrested ROFF for driving while disqualified. On the way to the station, ROFF began acting in a peculiar manner. When they arrived at the custody office, Constable McDONALD could not detect any signs that ROFF had been drinking. A short while later, the officer received information from a colleague that several canisters of butane gas had been found in ROFF's car.

Would Constable McDONALD now be entitled to arrest ROFF for an offence under s. 4 of the Road Traffic Act 1988?

A No, as butane gas is not a 'drug', and it is unlikely that the prosecution will be able show the quantity of it in ROFF's body.

5. Drink Driving

B No, because the officer formed the suspicion that ROFF was intoxicated after he had stopped driving his vehicle.

C No, because a constable may arrest a person under this section only when he or she is committing the offence.

D Yes, Constable McDONALD has reason to suspect that ROFF has committed an offence under s. 4 of the Act.

Question 5.4

ROBINSON was involved in an accident when driving home from the pub one evening. The police attended and asked him to provide a sample of breath, which proved to be positive. ROBINSON was charged with the offence, but at his court appearance he pleaded not guilty. His defence was that while he had been in the pub, his friends had bought him alcoholic drinks when he had asked for low-alcohol lager.

What is the court likely to decide in respect of the responsibility ROBINSON had to check the contents of the drinks he was given?

A He had some positive duty to check whether the drinks contained alcohol before consuming them.

B He had an absolute duty to check whether the drinks contained alcohol before consuming them.

C He had no duty to check the whether the drinks contained alcohol; the fault lay with his friends.

D The fact that he asked for low alcohol was sufficient and he had complied with his duty.

Question 5.5

Constable REID stopped ROBERTSON after he had driven through a red traffic light. Constable REID administered a breath test, which was negative. At this point, Constable REID did not form the opinion that ROBERTSON had been drinking and decided to issue a fixed penalty notice. As Constable REID was talking to ROBERTSON, she noticed that his speech was slurred and consequently formed the opinion that he was unfit to drive.

What should Constable REID now do in respect of ROBERTSON, under the Road Traffic Act 1988?

A Wait for 20 minutes, and then ask him to supply another sample of breath.

B Nothing, he has already supplied a sample of breath.

5. Drink Driving

C Arrest him under s. 4 (unfit to drive through drink or drugs).
D Ask him to supply another sample of breath immediately.

Question 5.6

Constable SIER was on foot patrol one night, when a vehicle drove past him with a defective headlamp. Constable SIER recognised the driver as being ERSKINE and contacted his control room to ask for the vehicle to be stopped by another officer. Constable WHEELAN was on patrol in uniform about 20 minutes later, when he saw ERSKINE walking along. The vehicle was nowhere in sight.

> Would Constable WHEELAN have the power to require a breath test from ERSKINE in these circumstances?

A Yes, but only if he suspects ERSKINE has alcohol in his body.
B Yes, because he has committed a moving traffic offence.
C No, because he did not see ERSKINE driving himself.
D No, because ERSKINE is no longer driving.

Question 5.7

Constable COURT was conducting her first breath test procedure, having stopped KAY, who was driving with a defective light. During the test, Constable COURT failed to hold down a button on the breath test device for the recommended amount of time. However, the reading still showed a positive breath result and Constable COURT arrested KAY.

> Has Constable COURT acted correctly in these circumstances?

A Yes, Constable COURT has acted correctly in the circumstances and the arrest is lawful.
B No, the arrest is unlawful, as Constable COURT made a mistake with the procedure.
C No, the arrest is unlawful, but this would not affect the result of the case if KAY provided a positive sample at the station.
D No, the arrest is unlawful, and KAY should have been made to take the test again.

Question 5.8

Constable TAYLOR was called to a collision in a shopping centre car park, which was open to the public. SINGH had reversed his car into the path of a dumper truck being

5. Drink Driving

driven by WALSH. WALSH was working on an adjacent building site and the dumper truck he was driving was not manufactured for use on roads.

> From whom, if anyone, may Constable TAYLOR require a breath test, in these circumstances?
>
> **A** SINGH only, provided she suspects he has alcohol in his body.
> **B** Neither driver, as the accident did not occur on a road.
> **C** Both drivers, as they have been involved in an accident.
> **D** SINGH only, whether or not she suspects he has alcohol in his body.

Question 5.9

Detective Constable PRINCE was in plain clothes, driving an unmarked police vehicle, when he saw DART, who was driving a motor car, collide with a pedal cyclist. The cycle was damaged as a result of the collision. DC PRINCE stopped to assist and as he was speaking to DART, he could smell intoxicants on his breath. DC PRINCE asked DART to provide a specimen of breath, but he had no device with him, nor did he have a radio to call for one. DC PRINCE asked DART to accompany him to the nearest police station to provide the specimen.

> Has DC PRINCE acted correctly in these circumstances?
>
> **A** No, he was not in uniform and had no power to demand a breath test.
> **B** No, he should have waited until he was at the station to request the specimen.
> **C** Yes, he has acted correctly in these circumstances.
> **D** No, the specimen should have been provided at the scene of the accident.

Question 5.10

Constable BARNETT, a probationer constable, approached his sergeant to discuss an initiative he had planned for the next set of night shifts. It was Constable BARNETT's intention to stop-check motor vehicles in the High Street at 11.30 pm on a Saturday night, in order to detect drink-driving offences.

> Would such an initiative be lawful under the Road Traffic Act 1988?
>
> **A** No, the police may only conduct random checks to establish the identity of drivers.
> **B** Yes, officers may stop vehicles in order to conduct random preliminary breath tests.
> **C** No, random checks such as this are contrary to a person's human rights.
> **D** Yes, officers may randomly check vehicles to enquire whether the driver has been drinking.

5. Drink Driving

Question 5.11

Constable MAY has stopped LENNARD, who had driven through a 'No Entry' sign late at night. Constable MAY asked LENNARD to supply a specimen of breath. LENNARD stated that he was unable to do so, as he had recently had heart surgery and the test might cause him to be seriously ill.

Would Constable MAY be entitled to arrest LENNARD for failing to supply a sample of breath?

A Yes, any person who refuses to supply a breath test may be arrested.
B Yes, but only if she suspects LENNARD has alcohol in his body.
C No, no further action should be taken because of LENNARD's illness.
D Yes, provided she suspects that LENNARD is over the prescribed limit.

Question 5.12

BALL drove his car into a garden wall and, without stopping, made his way home. He was alone in the car and no other people were involved. Constable DAWE arrived at the scene and, following a PNC check, attended BALL's home address. Constable DAWE found BALL in the front garden of his house and asked him for a sample of breath, as the officer suspected he had been involved in a road traffic accident. BALL refused and was arrested by the officer. BALL refused to go with Constable DAWE and told him to leave his property.

Does Constable DAWE have the power to continue with his arrest now that he has become a trespasser?

A Yes, BALL was arrested before Constable DAWE became a trespasser.
B Yes, Constable DAWE had a power to enter premises, as BALL had been involved in an accident.
C No, the arrest was unlawful, as Constable DAWE was trespassing as soon as he entered the garden.
D No, Constable DAWE has now become a trespasser and must leave the property.

Question 5.13

Section 6E of the Road Traffic Act 1988 provides a power of entry for a constable in certain circumstances.

Which of the following statements accurately sets out the relevant criteria that must apply before the power exists?

5. Drink Driving

A Reasonable belief that an accident has taken place; reasonable belief that the person was the driver; reasonable suspicion that it involved injury; reasonable suspicion that the person is on the premises.
B Reasonable suspicion that an accident has taken place; reasonable suspicion that the person was the driver; knowledge that it involved injury; reasonable suspicion that the driver is on the premises.
C Knowledge that an accident has taken place; reasonable belief that the person was the driver; reasonable suspicion that it involved injury; knowledge that the person is on the premises.
D Knowledge that an accident has taken place; reasonable belief that the person was the driver; reasonable suspicion that it involved injury; reasonable suspicion that the person is on the premises.

Question 5.14

Constable PENG is trained to conduct preliminary impairment tests. He was called to assist another officer who had stopped a motor vehicle, which was being driven erratically by WENGER. The officer had administered a breath test, which was negative; however, WENGER's behaviour led the officer to believe that he was under the influence of either drink or drugs. On his arrival, Constable PENG gave instructions to WENGER as part of the test, but WENGER was not able to complete the test because of his condition.

Would the officer be able to arrest WENGER now, for failure to complete the impairment test?

A Yes, provided the officer suspects the presence of alcohol or drugs.
B No, as he has not refused to take the impairment test.
C Yes, regardless of whether the officer suspects the presence of alcohol or drugs.
D No, the officer would have to arrest him under s. 4 of the Act.

Question 5.15

Constable COLE attended a road traffic accident involving a car which had struck a wall. There were two occupants in the vehicle: PEARSON, the owner, and his friend STUART. Constable COLE could smell intoxicants on both persons, but neither admitted being the driver of the vehicle at the time of the accident. PEARSON and STUART provided screening samples of breath, which were both positive. They were arrested and taken to the police station.

5. Drink Driving

From whom, if either, could a specimen of breath for analysis be requested, under s. 7 of the Road Traffic Act 1988 (provision of specimens for analysis)?
A Both, provided it is believed one of them was driving.
B PEARSON only, as the owner of the vehicle.
C Both, regardless of who was suspected to be the driver.
D Neither, Constable COLE should not have breathalysed both persons.

Question 5.16

Section 7 of the Road Traffic Act 1988 deals with the requirement to provide a specimen of breath for analysis (in respect of a person who is suspected of committing an offence under s. 3A, 4 or 5 of the Act).

Where may such a request be made of a suspected person, under s. 7?
A Anywhere, provided the sample is taken at a police station.
B At a police station or hospital only.
C Anywhere, provided the sample is taken at a police station or a hospital.
D At a police station only.

Question 5.17

Sergeant COWLEY was conducting the station breath test procedure for CATTON. CATTON was so drunk that Sergeant COWLEY feared he did not understand the procedure. As a precaution, Sergeant COWLEY called a police doctor to examine CATTON, believing there might be a medical reason for not providing a specimen of breath.

Has Sergeant COWLEY acted lawfully in these circumstances?
A No, he should have consulted the police doctor before deciding there was a medical reason preventing CATTON from providing a sample.
B No, he did not have reasonable cause to believe CATTON had a medical reason preventing him from providing a sample.
C Yes, Sergeant COWLEY has acted lawfully in these circumstances because of CATTON's condition.
D No, CATTON's drunkenness would not be a medical reason, which would prevent him from providing a sample.

5. Drink Driving

Question 5.18

Sergeant SWEENEY was conducting the station breath test procedure in relation to DENNY. DENNY provided one specimen of breath, which was over the prescribed limit. However, before he could provide a second specimen, the machine malfunctioned and Sergeant SWEENEY was unable to complete the procedure.

What action should Sergeant SWEENEY have taken in order to complete the station procedure?

A Request that DENNY provides a sample of blood or urine, and use that reading, together with the breath test reading as evidence.
B Charge DENNY with driving with excess alcohol, using the one reading as evidence that he was over the limit.
C The only option available to Sergeant SWEENEY is to request that DENNY provides a sample of blood to replace the reading.
D Sergeant SWEENEY may transfer DENNY to another station if there is another machine available.

Question 5.19

In which of the scenarios below, if any, will the custody officer have acted **incorrectly**, in respect of a requirement made under s. 7 of the Road Traffic Act 1988? (In each case the defendant has been arrested for providing a positive roadside breath test.)

1. The custody officer has requested a blood sample from THYNNE instead of two specimens of breath because the breath test machine is defective.
2. The custody officer has required BERRY to provide a blood sample for medical reasons, and has transferred him to another station, where a doctor is available.
3. The custody officer has requested a blood sample from KELLIHER, as there is no trained officer available to take specimens of breath.

A None of the above.
B Scenarios 1 and 3 only.
C Scenario 2 only.
D Scenarios 2 and 3 only.

Question 5.20

COLE was arrested for failing to provide a roadside breath test. On his arrival at the police station, COLE provided two samples of breath. Both readings were very low.

5. Drink Driving

However, the custody officer, Sergeant WONG, believed that COLE may have taken drugs as he was exhibiting similar behaviour to a drunken person.

What would be the correct course of action for Sergeant WONG to take in these circumstances?

A Consult a doctor, who must confirm writing that COLE's behaviour is due to his taking drugs and then request a sample of blood or urine.
B Request a blood or urine sample from COLE and then call a doctor to take either the blood sample or urine sample.
C Consult a doctor, who must confirm verbally that COLE's behaviour is due to his taking drugs and then request a sample of blood or urine.
D Request a blood or urine sample from COLE and then call a doctor to take the sample, if it is blood, or take the sample himself if it is urine.

Question 5.21

Under s. 7(4) of the Road Traffic Act 1988, a specimen of blood or urine may be required from a person in custody.

In relation to this provision, who will decide which specimen is to be obtained from such a person?

A It will always be the officer's decision, and there is no requirement to consult on this issue.
B It will always be the officer's decision, unless the driver objects; then a doctor will rule on the validity of the objection.
C The driver must be given a choice as to whether he or she would like to give blood or urine.
D It will always be the officer's decision, unless the driver objects; then it will be a joint decision in consultation with a doctor.

Question 5.22

When a constable is requesting the provision of a specimen under s. 7(7) of the Road Traffic Act 1988, a warning must be given that a failure to provide the specimen may render a person liable to prosecution.

Who is responsible for giving the warning under s. 7(7)?

A It must be given by the person requesting the specimen.
B It may be given by any officer not involved in the arrest.
C It must be given by the custody officer, or the person requesting the specimen.
D It may be given by any officer.

5. Drink Driving

Question 5.23

KHAN has provided two specimens of breath during the station breath test procedure, the readings being 49 and 50 respectively. Sergeant WILSON informed KHAN that he could replace the samples with blood or urine. KHAN stated that he would prefer not to give blood, as he had a fear of needles. Sergeant WILSON has been informed that a doctor is available by telephone only and will not attend immediately.

What action should Sergeant WILSON now take in respect of KHAN?

A Speak to the doctor on the telephone and proceed as advised by him or her.
B Request a sample of blood if necessary; a fear of needles is not a medical reason for not giving blood.
C Take a sample of urine from KHAN, as the choice is his as to which sample may be taken.
D Wait until the doctor arrives and proceed as advised by him or her; such advice may not be taken by telephone.

Question 5.24

JONES was arrested following a positive roadside breath test and taken to a police station. He provided a further two samples of breath, the readings being 48 and 47 respectively. JONES later provided a specimen of blood, which was divided and a portion given to him. The arresting officer received notification a few weeks later that an error had occurred with the sample forwarded for analysis, and that it could not be used in evidence.

What options are now open to the arresting officer, in order to proceed against JONES for the offence of driving with excess alcohol?

A Both breath specimens may be used as evidence to prosecute JONES for the offence.
B JONES may be prosecuted, using the lower reading as evidence.
C JONES may not be prosecuted in these circumstances; the case must be dismissed.
D The lower reading may be used as evidence, and the court must decide on the balance of probabilities if he is guilty.

5. Drink Driving

Question 5.25

Sergeant DONELLY was conducting the station breath test procedure for BEECH, who had provided one sample of breath. However, BEECH stated that he was tired, and fell asleep before providing a second sample. Sergeant DONELLY tried to wake BEECH, without success, and in the end placed him in a cell. BEECH was later charged with driving with excess alcohol, based on the reading provided, which was 150 microgrammes of alcohol in 100 millilitres of breath.

Has Sergeant DONELLY acted correctly in these circumstances?

A Yes, Sergeant DONELLY has acted correctly in these circumstances as BEECH has driven with excess alcohol.
B No, BEECH should have been charged with failing to provide a sample, but his drunken condition may provide a defence.
C No, BEECH should have been given the opportunity to provide a sample of blood or urine when he was sober enough.
D No, BEECH should have been charged with failing to provide a sample and would have no defence arising from his drunken condition.

Question 5.26

In which of the following scenarios has it been held that a person does not have a reasonable excuse for failing to provide a specimen under s. 7 of the Road Traffic Act 1988?
1. The defendant refused to supply a specimen because he or she believed that the officer did not have the authority to ask for one.
2. The defendant refused to supply a specimen because he or she could not understand what was being said due to a language barrier.
3. The defendant refused to supply a specimen until he or she had spoken to a solicitor.
4. The defendant refused to supply a specimen until he or she had read the Codes of Practice under the Police and Criminal Evidence Act 1984.

A All of the above.
B Scenarios 1, 2 and 4 only.
C Scenarios 3 and 4 only.
D Scenarios 1, 3 and 4 only.

5. Drink Driving

Question 5.27

In which of the following scenarios, if either, will the person have failed to provide a specimen for analysis, without 'reasonable excuse', under s. 7(6) of the Road Traffic Act 1988?

1. HIGGINS has consented to provide a specimen of blood, but only if it is taken from his left arm.
2. DICKESON consented to providing a specimen of urine, but was able to urinate only once. He has refused to provide a second sample, stating that the one he has provided may be split in two.

A Scenario 1 only.
B Scenario 2 only.
C Both scenarios.
D Neither scenario.

Question 5.28

Section 7(5) of the Road Traffic Act 1988 sets out the time period during which a person must provide two samples of urine while in police detention.

What is the time period referred to?

A One hour from the time that the station breath test procedure was completed.
B Two hours from the time the request was made.
C One hour from the time the request was made.
D No time limit, but the samples must be produced within a reasonable time.

Question 5.29

MILLARD was charged with causing death by careless driving, whilst unfit drive through drugs. MILLARD proposed to introduce evidence in court to prove that she had not been under the influence of drugs at the time of the alleged offence. MILLARD contested that she had taken drugs after she had ceased to drive her car, and was no longer in charge of it.

What effect will this have on the court's ability to make an assumption, under s. 15 of the Road Traffic Offenders Act 1988, that the proportion of drugs in MILLARD's body was the same at the time of the accident as when she later provided the sample?

A The court will take into account any sample provided by MILLARD only if the prosecution can discredit her evidence.

5. Drink Driving

B None, the court would not have been able to make that assumption as MILLARD was not under the influence of alcohol.
C None, the assumption under s. 15 does not apply to the offence that MILLARD is alleged to have committed.
D None, only the prosecution may introduce such evidence and since they have not, the court must take into account the sample.

Question 5.30

Section 15(5) of the Road Traffic Offenders Act 1988, deals with the provision of a specimen to the accused, which has been taken from him or her.

In relation to the provision of such a sample, which of the following statements will be correct?

A It must be provided in every case to the defendant at the time it was taken, after it has been divided in his or her presence.
B It must be provided when requested by the defendant, not necessarily at the time it was taken, and it need not be divided in his or her presence.
C It must be provided in every case to the defendant at the time it was taken, but it need not be divided in his or her presence.
D It must be provided when requested by the defendant at the time it was taken, after it has been divided in his or her presence.

Question 5.31

MALIK was arrested following a positive roadside breath test. Constable SWEENEY conducted the station procedure and MALIK provided a further two specimens of breath for analysis, which were positive. The breath test machine produced a certificate of the breath test readings, together with two copies.

What documentary evidence must MALIK be provided with, in these circumstances?

A The original certificate, signed by Constable SWEENEY.
B A copy of the certificate, unsigned.
C Two copies of the certificate, one signed by Constable SWEENEY.
D A copy of the certificate, signed by Constable SWEENEY.

5. Drink Driving

Question 5.32

NEWMAN is in custody and is suspected of being unfit to drive through taking drugs. NEWMAN has provided a specimen of blood, which the custody officer, Sergeant BURKE, intends to submit for analysis. NEWMAN will not be charged until the results of the analysis are known and, therefore, Sergeant BURKE intends to release him on bail for the period. However, NEWMAN has stated his intention to drive when released. Sergeant BURKE suspects that NEWMAN would still be unfit if he were to drive a motor vehicle on a road.

What does s. 10 of the Road Traffic Act 1988 say, in relation to the advice Sergeant BURKE should seek, before detaining NEWMAN further until he is fit to drive a motor vehicle on a road?

A   Sergeant BURKE may make this decision herself; she does not need to seek advice from anyone.
B   Sergeant BURKE may seek advice from a doctor, and must act on any advice given.
C   Sergeant BURKE may not detain NEWMAN under this section, as he has not been charged or reported with an offence.
D   Sergeant BURKE must seek advice from a doctor, and must act on any advice given.

Question 5.33

ASKEW was involved in a road traffic accident during which she received head injuries, and was taken to hospital. The officer dealing with the accident, Constable LEE, was told by witnesses that ASKEW's driving was erratic immediately prior to the accident. Constable LEE attended the hospital to interview ASKEW and require her to provide a sample of breath. On his arrival, Constable LEE was told that ASKEW was unconscious due to her injuries. Constable LEE considered that a sample of blood should be taken from ASKEW without her permission.

Who would be able to take such a sample from ASKEW, under s. 7A of the Road Traffic Act 1988?

A   A police medical practitioner or the medical practitioner in charge of the patient.
B   A police medical practitioner or any other medical practitioner, but not the one in charge of the patient.
C   A police medical practitioner only.

D A police medical practitioner, the medical practitioner in charge of the patient or a registered health care professional.

Question 5.34

WEBBER was at a hospital, having been involved in a road traffic accident. Having consulted with WEBBER's doctor, Constable O'SHEA required WEBBER to provide a specimen of breath, but she refused. Constable O'SHEA arrested WEBBER for failing to provide a specimen. After further consultation with the doctor, Constable O'SHEA asked WEBBER to supply a specimen of blood.

Has Constable O'SHEA complied with the requirements of s. 9 of the Road Traffic Act 1988?

A No, because WEBBER was under arrest, the request for blood should have been made at a police station.
B No, he should not have arrested WEBBER while she was still a patient at the hospital.
C Yes, as the doctor has agreed to both specimens being requested, he has complied with the Act.
D Yes, but there was no need to ask permission on the second occasion, as permission had already been granted.

5. Drink Driving

ANSWERS

Answer 5.1

Answer **C** — Section 4(6) of the Road Traffic Act 1988 provides that a constable may arrest a person without warrant if he or she has reasonable cause to suspect that they have committed an offence under s. 4. For the purpose of *arresting* a person under the power conferred by s. 4(6), a constable may enter, if need be by force, *any place* where that person is or with reasonable cause is suspected to be (s. 4(7)). Answer B is incorrect as the power is provided to enter to *arrest* a person, not to breathalise. Answer D is incorrect as the power is available to enter any *place* where the person is.

Evidence of impairment must be produced by the prosecution, and that evidence may be provided by a 'lay' witness, provided that witness is not required to give expert testimony or to comment on the defendant's ability to drive (*R* v *Lanfear* [1968] 2 QB 77). Answer A is therefore incorrect.

Road Traffic, paras 3.5.2.1, 3.5.2.2

Answer 5.2

Answer **A** — Section 5(2) of the Road Traffic Act 1988 provides a defence for a person charged with an offence under s. 5(1)(b) (in charge of a motor vehicle whilst over the prescribed limit), provided there was no likelihood of him or her driving the vehicle whilst unfit.

The situation was examined recently by the Divisional Court, in the case of *Sheldrake* v *DPP* [2003] 2 All ER 497. The defendant claimed that the application of s. 5(2) above was contrary to Article 6(2) of the European Convention on Human Rights, (presumption of innocence). The court held that s. 5(2) *did not* breach Article 6(2), and that a person charged with an offence under s. 5(1)(b) above must *demonstrate from the evidence an arguable case that* there was no likelihood of him driving whilst unfit to do so. Answer C is therefore incorrect.

The prosecution do have a responsibility under s. 5(2) above, to show beyond reasonable doubt that there *was* a likelihood of the defendant driving, *but **only if** the defendant has first presented a successful argument as referred to above*. Since the initial responsibility lies with the defendant, answers B and D are incorrect.

Road Traffic, para. 3.5.3.1

Answer 5.3

Answer **D** — 'Drugs' for the purpose of s. 4 of the Road Traffic Act 1988 will include any intoxicant other than alcohol (s. 11), and will include *toluene* found in some glues (*Bradford* v *Wilson* (1983) 78 Cr App R 77). As the effects of butane gas can be 'intoxicating', this will be included as an intoxicant. Unlike offences under s. 5, it is not necessary under s. 4 to show what quantity of alcohol or drug the defendant had in his or her system to convict of the offence. Answer A is therefore incorrect.

The suspicion need not be formed while the defendant is driving and can become apparent after he or she has been stopped or spoken to for some other reason (*R* v *Roff* [1976] RTR 7). Answer B is therefore incorrect.

A constable may arrest without warrant any person he or she has reasonable cause to suspect *is* committing an offence *or has been* committing an offence (s. 4(6)). Answer C is therefore incorrect.

Road Traffic, paras 3.5.2.1, 3.5.2.2

Answer 5.4

Answer **A** — The facts in this question are taken from *Robinson* v *DPP* [2003] EWHC 2718. In that case, the Divisional Court held that a person is under *some positive duty* to check whether drinks contained alcohol before consuming them, if the person intends to drive afterwards. Answers B, C and D are therefore incorrect.

Road Traffic, para. 3.5.3

Answer 5.5

Answer **C** — Under s. 4 of the Road Traffic Act 1988, a constable may arrest without warrant any person whom he or she has reasonable cause to suspect has been driving a mechanically propelled vehicle on a road, while unfit to do so through drink or drugs.

There is no requirement under this section to have administered a breath test before the power of arrest is utilised. The circumstances in the question mirror those in the case of *DPP* v *Robertson* [2002] RTR 383. In this case, the Administrative Court decided that even though the driver had provided a negative screening test, he was seen moments later staggering in a way which gave rise to a suspicion of unfitness. In such a case, s. 4 of the Act gave the officer reasonable cause to suspect that the person

5. Drink Driving

was impaired, which in turn meant that an arrest would be lawful. Answers A, B and D are therefore incorrect.

Road Traffic, para. 3.5.2.1

Answer 5.6

Answer **B** — Sections 6(4)(a)–(b) of the Road Traffic Act 1988 state that a preliminary breath test may be required if a constable reasonably suspects that the person is or has been driving or attempting to drive, or is or has been in charge of a motor vehicle on a road or other public place and has committed a traffic offence while the vehicle was in motion. Answer D is incorrect, as the test may be required as the driver *was* driving while committing a moving traffic offence.

Where the person is suspected of committing an offence while the vehicle was in motion, there is no requirement for the officer to suspect that he or she has alcohol in his or her body, or still has alcohol in his or her body when making the request (this is in contrast to the requirements under s. 6(2) and (3) of the 1988 Act of driving/attempting to drive or being in charge). Answer A is therefore incorrect.

One officer's 'reasonable cause to suspect' may arise from the observations of another officer (*Erskine* v *Hollin* [1971] RTR 199). Answer C is therefore incorrect.

Road Traffic, paras 3.5.4, 3.5.4.1

Answer 5.7

Answer **A** — It has been held that where a constable innocently fails to follow the manufacturer's instructions, it will not render the test nor any subsequent arrest unlawful (*DPP* v *Kay* [1999] RTR 109). Answer B is therefore incorrect. Answer C is also incorrect, as the arrest was not unlawful.

In addition to the case of *Kay* above, it was decided in *DPP* v *Carey* [1969] 3 All ER 1662, that failing to comply with the manufacturer's instructions on the use of an approved device will mean that the person *has not provided* a preliminary breath test and *may* be asked to provide another; refusing to do so will be an offence. Answer D is incorrect, as the case is not the authority for the view that a person *must* be made to take another test. Since the purpose of the test is to indicate whether there is a *likelihood* of an offence being committed, an arrest in these circumstances is appropriate, as the test did show a positive result.

Road Traffic, para. 3.5.4.2

5. Drink Driving

Answer 5.8

Answer **D** — The power to conduct a breath test under s. 6(5) of the Road Traffic Act 1988 applies where an accident has occurred owing to the presence of a *motor vehicle* on a *road or public place*. Since Walsh was driving a *mechanically propelled vehicle* and not a *motor vehicle*, there is no power to request a breath test from him. Answer C is therefore incorrect. As s. 6 applies to accidents that occur in a *public place* as well as on a road, answer B is also incorrect.

There is no need for the officer making the enquiry to suspect or believe that the driver has been drinking, nor that he has committed an offence in order to require a breath test following an accident. Answer A is therefore incorrect.

Road Traffic, para. 3.5.4.3

Answer 5.9

Answer **C** — Section 6(5) of the Road Traffic Act 1988 provides that following an accident involving a motor vehicle on a road, a *constable* may require the driver to provide a specimen of breath for a breath test. The section does not require the officer to be in uniform. Answer A is therefore incorrect.

The specimen after an accident may be taken *at or near* the place where the requirement is made (answer D is therefore incorrect). If the officer making the requirement thinks it expedient, he or she may request that it be provided at a police station specified by that officer. There is no need for the officer to wait until he or she arrives at the station to make the requirement. Answer B is therefore incorrect.

Road Traffic, para. 3.5.4.3

Answer 5.10

Answer **D** — The police are empowered to stop vehicles at random (under s. 163 of the Road Traffic Act 1998) to establish the identity of the driver, to enquire whether the driver has been drinking, or to train newly appointed officers in traffic procedures (see *Chief Constable of Gwent* v *Dash* [1986] RTR 41). Answers A and C are therefore incorrect.

However, this case does not allow officers to conduct random preliminary breath tests, which means that answer B is incorrect. The difference between answers B and D is that under answer B, officers would be stopping vehicles and administering breath tests to any driver, whether they had good cause to do so or not. This is clearly not acceptable within the framework of the Human Rights Act 1998. It should be

5. Drink Driving

noted, however, that having stopped a vehicle at random correctly, there is nothing to prevent the driver from being asked to provide a sample of breath if the officer suspects the presence of alcohol or drugs.

Road Traffic, para. 3.5.4

Answer 5.11

Answer **B** — A person who fails to co-operate with a preliminary sample *without reasonable excuse* is guilty of an offence under s. 6 of the Road Traffic Act 1988. A person would have a 'reasonable excuse' if he or she was physically unable to provide a sample, if to do so would represent a substantial risk to his or her health (*R v Lennard* [1973] 2 All ER 831). Clearly, where a person has a severe heart condition, as in the question, this might be a reasonable excuse.

However, this does not mean that the police can take no further action. This is merely a defence that the defendant may use to a charge of failing to provide a sample. If the officer suspects that the person has alcohol in his or her body, he or she should not release the person to drive away! The person may be arrested in order to go through the station procedure and he or she may provide a blood or urine sample as an alternative. Answer C is therefore incorrect.

Section 6D(1) of the 1988 Act provides a power of arrest where a person has failed to provide a preliminary breath test, and the constable reasonably suspects that the *person has alcohol in his or her body*. Answer A is incorrect as the power is given provisionally and not every person who fails to co-operate will be arrested. Note that the constable must reasonably suspect that the driver has *alcohol in his or her body*, in order to exercise the power of arrest. It is not essential that the constable suspects the person is over the prescribed limit at this point, which is why answer D is incorrect.

Road Traffic, paras 3.5.4.4, 3.5.4.7

Answer 5.12

Answer **A** — Generally, where an officer is trespassing on a defendant's property, he or she is not entitled to require a breath test (*R v Fox* [1986] AC 281). Also, if officers are trespassing, any subsequent arrest made by them is unlawful (*Clowser* v *Chaplin* [1981] RTR 317). However, any requirement for a sample of breath properly made and any subsequent arrest remains lawful *until* the officer becomes a trespasser.

A police officer, like any other citizen, has an implied licence to go on to certain parts of property (which might include a garden), unless and until that licence is

5. Drink Driving

withdrawn. It is when the licence is withdrawn that the officer may become a trespasser. Therefore, if a police officer is on the defendant's property and has not been told to leave, any requirement for a breath test and subsequent arrest is lawful (*Pamplin* v *Fraser* [1981] RTR 494). This would still be the case even if the licence were withdrawn later. Answer D is therefore incorrect.

In the scenario given, the officer was not a trespasser until the defendant told him to leave the garden. Answer C is therefore incorrect.

Constable DAWE has no statutory power to enter the premises under s. 6D of the Road Traffic Act 1988, as this section only affords a power of entry following an accident involving *injury* to a person other than the driver. Answer B is incorrect as the scenario did not involve an injury.

Road Traffic, para. 3.5.4.5

Answer 5.13

Answer **D** — Under s. 6E of the Road Traffic Act 1988, a constable may enter premises to carry out a preliminary breath test, to arrest a person following such a test and to arrest a person who has failed to supply such a test.

Before the power is used, there are *four* criteria that *must* apply. The officer must:

- *know* that an accident has taken place (mere suspicion is not enough);
- have *reasonable cause to believe* that the person had been driving or attempting to drive, or had been in charge of the vehicle (mere suspicion is not enough);
- have *reasonable cause to suspect* that the accident involved injury to another person (here suspicion is enough); *and*
- have *reasonable cause to suspect* that the person he or she is seeking is in the place to be entered (again suspicion is enough).

Answer D is the only option with all the correct criteria in place, and therefore answers A, B and C are incorrect.

Road Traffic, para. 3.5.4.6

Answer 5.14

Answer **A** — Under s. 6B of the Road Traffic Act 1988, an appropriately trained officer has the power to require the driver of a motor vehicle on a road or public place to submit to a preliminary impairment test, to observe the driver's behaviour. Such observations may be used as evidence in any subsequent court cases — but will not provide absolute proof of a person's guilt.

5. Drink Driving

A person who fails to co-operate with a preliminary impairment test commits an offence under s. 6(6) of the Act. A person does not co-operate unless his or her co-operation is sufficient to allow the test to be carried out (s. 11(3)). In the question, the driver's behaviour meant that the test could not be carried out, even though he did not refuse to take it. Answer B is therefore incorrect.

A constable may arrest a person who has failed to co-operate with a test under this section, *provided* the constable reasonably suspects that the person has alcohol or drugs in his or her body, or is under the influence of drugs (s. 6D(2)). Answers C and D are therefore incorrect.

Road Traffic, paras 3.5.4.2, 3.5.4.4, 3.5.4.7

Answer 5.15

Answer **A** — It was held in the case of *Pearson v Metropolitan Police Commissioner* [1988] RTR 276, that the requirement under s. 7 may be made of more than one person (in this instance three people were involved), in respect of the same vehicle. Answers B and D are therefore incorrect. However, it must be believed that one of them was driving the vehicle, and answer C is incorrect.

Road Traffic, para. 3.5.5.2

Answer 5.16

Answer **D** — Section 7(2) of the Road Traffic Act 1988 is specific as to where the request for a breath specimen may be *made*. The request may **only** be made at a police station, and answers A, B and C are incorrect. Logically, a police station is the only place where such a specimen may be taken, as this is where the breath test machine is kept!

Road Traffic, para. 3.5.5.2

Answer 5.17

Answer **C** — For the officer to have 'reasonable cause to *believe*' that a medical reason exists, there is no need to seek medical advice first (*Dempsey v Catton* [1986] RTR 194). Answer A is therefore incorrect.

It is the objective *cause* of the belief that a medical reason exists that will be considered by the courts, not whether the officer actually did believe that a medical reason existed (*Davis v DPP* [1988 RTR 156). Therefore, the officer's precautionary measures were appropriate.

5. Drink Driving

Practically, custody officers are often faced with this dilemma, as suspects may attempt to confuse the issue by feigning illness. Evidentially, nothing will be lost if a sample of blood is obtained, and it is often better to err on the side of caution, particularly when there is case law such as *Davis* as a fallback. Answer B is therefore incorrect.

If a person is too drunk to provide a breath specimen, that may be regarded as a 'medical reason' for requiring a sample of blood or urine (*Young* v *DPP* [1992] RTR 328). Answer D is therefore incorrect.

Note that the power to take a blood sample in these circumstances has been extended to a 'registered health care professional'.

Road Traffic, para. 3.5.5.3

Answer 5.18

Answer **D** — If the machine being used at one station is unreliable, by virtue of the fact that it will not calibrate the reading correctly, it will be 'unavailable'. In this case, the driver may be taken to another station, where another machine is available, *even if the driver has already provided two samples on the inaccurate machine* (*Denny* v *DPP* [1990] RTR 417). Answer D is correct for this reason.

The prosecution may not use a breath test reading *and* a blood reading in the same case. If a requirement to provide blood/urine is made, that sample must be used and the prosecution may not revert to the evidence produced by the breath sample. In effect the blood sample replaces the breath sample (*Badkin* v *Chief Constable of South Yorkshire* [1988] RTR 401). Answer A is therefore incorrect.

Answer B is incorrect as two specimens of breath must be submitted as evidence to the court. It has been held that if the defendant supplies one specimen only, this will be deemed a failure to provide.

Under s. 7(3)(b) of the Road Traffic Act 1988, the defendant *may* be asked to provide a sample of blood/urine, where the device is unavailable for breath tests. However, the case of *Denny* above shows that this is not the only option available. Answer C is therefore incorrect.

Road Traffic, para. 3.5.5.4

Answer 5.19

Answer **A** — All scenarios are taken from decided cases in relation to procedure under s. 7 of the Road Traffic Act 1988, where officers have been found by the courts to have acted correctly.

5. Drink Driving

In the case of *Thompson* v *Thynne* [1986] Crim LR 629, the court held that where an officer knew at the time that the breath test machine was unavailable due to a malfunction, he or she could require a specimen of blood/urine.

In the case of *Chief Constable of Kent* v *Berry* [1986] Crim LR 748, it was decided that the driver may be taken to another police station where a doctor is available. (This power extends to a registered health care professional.)

In the case of *Chief Constable of Avon and Somerset* v *Kelliher* [1986] Crim LR 635, it was decided that where no trained officer was available to operate the machine, it will be 'unavailable' and a specimen of blood/urine may be requested.

Consequently, answers B, C and D are incorrect.

Road Traffic, para. 3.5.5.4

Answer 5.20

Answer **C** — Where it is suspected that the driver of a vehicle, who has been requested to provide a sample under s. 7 of the Road Traffic Act 1988, is under the influence of drugs, the advice of a medical practitioner *must* be sought *before* the request is made to provide blood or urine (s. 7(3)(c)). Answers B and D are both incorrect in this respect. Answer B is also incorrect in relation to procedure, because where a person has been asked to provide a specimen of urine, there is no requirement for a medical practitioner to take the sample — it may be taken by a police officer.

When medical advice is sought in these circumstances, the doctor must give the officer a 'clear verbal' statement to the effect that the driver's condition was due to some drug, *before* the request is made for blood/urine (*Cole* v *DPP* [1988] RTR 224). Answer A is therefore incorrect.

Note the extended power given to registered health care professionals to take blood.

Road Traffic, para. 3.5.5.5

Answer 5.21

Answer **B** — The House of Lords ruling in the case of *DPP* v *Warren* [1993] AC 319 ended many arguments in relation to whether the driver should be given a preference as to whether he or she gave blood or urine. Their Lordships stated unequivocally that the decision must be made by the officer. Answer C is incorrect, as the driver is not given a choice in these matters. However, this is not to say that the officer should take no notice of information given by the driver. The discretion given

5. Drink Driving

to the officer must be exercised reasonably (see *Joseph & DPP* [2003] *The Times*, 2 December).

There will be occasions when a driver will legitimately be unable to provide a sample of blood for medical reasons. In the case of *DPP v Jackson; Stanley v DPP* [1998] 3 WLR 514, the House of Lords stressed the distinction between the role of the police officer and the doctor.

The police officer will decide *which* evidential sample should be obtained and the medical practitioner decides on the *validity of the reasons put forward by the defendant* as to why a specimen of blood should not be taken. Taking this decision a step further, the role of the officer will be to act on the 'advice' given by the doctor. Answer A is incorrect because there must be some consultation; and answer D is incorrect, as the *Stanley* case clearly shows a distinction between the decision makers — it is not a joint role.

Note the extended power given to registered health care professionals to take blood.

Road Traffic, para. 3.5.5.7

Answer 5.22

Answer **D** — It was held in the case of *Bobin v DPP* [1999] RTR 375 that as long as the warning is given to the person by a police officer, it does not matter *which* officer gives it. Therefore, under s. 7(7), the warning may be given by the person requiring the sample, the custody officer or even the officer in the case. For evidential purposes, the person giving the warning should make a note that this was done.

Consequently, answers A, B and C are incorrect.

Road Traffic, para. 3.5.5.7

Answer 5.23

Answer **A** — When the person has provided two samples, and the lower reading is below 50 microgrammes of alcohol in 100 millilitres of breath, the person who has provided the sample may replace the breath sample with either a specimen of blood or urine (s. 8(1) and (2) of the Road Traffic Act 1988). Although the defendant is given the choice as to whether he or she wishes to replace his or her sample, the choice as to which sample will be provided will be that of the officer. Answer C is therefore incorrect.

As with s. 7 of the 1988 Act, the possibility of medical reasons for not providing blood *must* be considered. An alleged fear of needles by the driver is a relevant

5. Drink Driving

consideration when making this decision (*DPP* v *Jackson; Stanley* v *DPP* [1998] 3 WLR 514 and also *Johnson* v *West Yorkshire Metropolitan Police* [1986] RTR 167). Answer B is therefore incorrect.

The medical advice may be given to the officer over the telephone if appropriate (*Andrews* v *DPP* [1992] RTR 1). Answer D is therefore incorrect.

Note the extended power given to registered health care professionals to take blood.

Road Traffic, para. 3.5.6.1

Answer 5.24

Answer **C** — When a fault occurs, which leads to a blood specimen being unsuitable, the prosecution may *not* use the original breath specimens to prove the person was over the limit (*Archbold* v *Jones* [1985] Crim LR 740). Answers A, B and D are therefore incorrect.

Road Traffic, para. 3.5.6.1

Answer 5.25

Answer **D** — Sergeant DONELLY has *not* acted correctly in these circumstances. Where a driver provides one specimen only, and fails without a reasonable excuse to provide the second sample, he or she has committed the offence of 'failing to provide' a sample (*Cracknell* v *Willis* [1987] 3 All ER 801). Answers A and C are incorrect for this reason.

'Mental impairment' may provide a reasonable excuse for failing to provide a sample. However, being drunk or under stress is not in itself enough to provide a 'reasonable excuse' for failing to provide a specimen (*DPP* v *Falzarano* [2001] RTR 14). This is confirmed by the case of *DPP* v *Beech* [1992] Crim LR 64, where it was decided that where the defendant's mental capacity to understand the warning was impaired by his or her drunkenness, this was not a 'reasonable' excuse. Answer B is therefore incorrect.

Road Traffic, para. 3.5.6.1

Answer 5.26

Answer **D** — What amounts to a 'reasonable excuse' is a matter of law. However, it has been left for the courts to decide whether or not a defendant *had* a reasonable excuse, having regard to the circumstances in each case. There is a long list in *Blackstone's Road Traffic Manual* identifying what will *not* amount to a 'reasonable excuse'. There are few examples of what *will* amount to a 'reasonable excuse' and these centre around physical and mental incapacity and the ability to understand because of *non-self-induced* matters (i.e. language barriers).

Scenario 2 is the only option out of the four where a person might be said to have a reasonable excuse. It would seem that this particular problem could be avoided under s. 7 of the Road Traffic Act 1988, if the Codes of Practice under Police and Criminal Evidence Act 1984, in relation to detention of persons in custody, are followed. The need for an interpreter should have been identified *before* the station procedure was carried out (this might be different in relation to roadside breath tests of course!).

Scenarios 1, 3 and 4 have been held *not* to be 'reasonable excuses'. It has been the author's experience that many 'delaying tactics' are used in respect of specimens and scenarios 3 and 4 are not uncommon. In practice, if the custody officer has time, and there is one readily available, allowing a person to speak to his or her solicitor can often be a worthwhile exercise, so long as the process is not held up for an unreasonable time. (Allowing the defendant to read the Codes of Practice may take a little longer!).

Consequently, answers A, B and C are incorrect.

Road Traffic, para. 3.5.6.1

Answer 5.27

Answer **C** — Both scenarios are taken from decided cases and are both examples of failing to provide specimens without a 'reasonable excuse'.

Scenario 1 reinforces the fact that consent may not be accompanied by 'conditions' laid down by the defendant. In *Rushton* v *Higgins* [1972] RTR 456, it was decided that once consent is given to provide a sample of blood, it is for the doctor to say from which part of the body it will be taken. Any insistence on a different course of action will be a refusal.

In relation to scenario 2, samples of urine will be admissible as long as they are provided within the time set out under s. 7(5) of the Road Traffic Act 1988 and that there are two distinct samples (as opposed to two samples taken during the same act of urinating) (*Prosser* v *Dickeson* [1982] RTR 96).

Consequently, answers A, B and D are incorrect.

Road Traffic, paras 3.5.7.1, 3.5.7.2

5. Drink Driving

Answer 5.28

Answer **C** — The samples must be produced under s. 7(5) within *one* hour *from the time the request was made*. Answers A, B and D are therefore incorrect.

Road Traffic, para. 3.5.7.2

Answer 5.29

Answer **B** — Under s. 15(2) of the Road Traffic Offenders Act 1988, the court *must* take into account any evidence of the proportion of alcohol or drugs in any specimen supplied by the accused.

However, s. 15(2) goes on to say that the court *must* assume that the proportion of *alcohol* in the accused's body at the time of the alleged offence was *not less* that the specimen provided (in other words at least the same). This assumption *does not* apply in cases where the defendant is alleged to have taken drugs. Answer B is correct for this reason.

Section 15(3) states that the accused may introduce evidence that he or she had consumed alcohol between the alleged driving offence and the provision of the specimen and that if he or she had not done so, the proportion of *alcohol* in his or her sample would not have exceeded the prescribed limit. Answer D is incorrect as this evidence *is* introduced by the *defence*.

However, as subsection (3) applies to the introduction of such evidence in cases involving *alcohol* only, it would not be applicable in the circumstances outlined. As this will not affect the ruling that the court must *take evidence into account* of the sample provided, answer A is incorrect.

This section applies to offences under s. 3A, 4 or 5 of the Road Traffic Act 1988. MILLARD is accused of an offence under s. 3A and therefore answer C is incorrect.

Road Traffic, para. 3.5.8

Answer 5.30

Answer **B** — The question deals with three elements of the provision of samples to the defendant: providing a sample on request and the timing of when the sample is divided and actually given to the defendant. Only answer B contains the correct statements for all three elements. The other answers contain a mixture of correct and incorrect statements. The correct statements are shown below.

Section 15(5) of the Road Traffic Offenders Act 1988 states that it must be shown that the defendant was supplied with a specimen *if he or she asked for one*.

5. Drink Driving

Although the specimen must be divided 'at the time', there is no need for it to be done in the defendant's presence (*DPP* v *Elstob* [1992] Crim LR 518).

Although the specimen must be divided at the time, there is no need to provide the defendant with his or her part 'at the time'. This may be done within a 'reasonable time' thereafter (*R* v *Sharp* [1968] 2 QB 564).

Consequently, answers A, C and D are incorrect.

Road Traffic, para. 3.5.8.4

Answer 5.31

Answer **B** — Section 16 of the Road Traffic Offenders Act 1988 deals with documentary evidence in relation to the taking of specimens of breath, blood or urine. The defendant must be provided with a *copy* of any statement produced by the breath test machine. Answer A is therefore incorrect.

However, it has been held that there is no requirement for the *copy* to be signed by a police officer (*Chief Constable of Surrey* v *Wickens* [1985] RTR 277). Consequently, answers C and D are incorrect.

Road Traffic, para. 3.5.8.5

Answer 5.32

Answer **D** — Section 10 of the Road Traffic Act 1988 allows for the detention of a person who has provided a specimen of breath, blood or urine, until it appears to a constable that were the person to drive a mechanically propelled vehicle on a road, he or she would not be committing an offence. The power does not apply if it appears to a constable that there is no likelihood of the person driving such a vehicle on a road. There is no mention of a person having been charged or reported for an offence, merely that they have been required to provide the relevant sample. Answer C is therefore incorrect.

Under s. 10(3), a constable *must* consult a medical practitioner on *any question arising under this section whether a person's ability to drive properly is or might be impaired through drugs*. The constable *must* act on such advice. This is mandatory; therefore, both answers A and B are incorrect.

Road Traffic, para. 3.5.9

5. Drink Driving

Answer 5.33

Answer **B** — The power under s. 7A of the Road Traffic Act 1988 allows a sample of blood to be taken from a person without his or her consent, at a hospital. It may be taken if the driver has been 'involved' in an accident and is incapable of giving consent because he or she is incapacitated due to medical reasons.

Section 7A(2)(a) states that a request under *this section* shall not be made to a medical practitioner 'who for the time being has any responsibility for the clinical care of the person concerned'. **Note**, however, that the medical practitioner in charge of the patient must *still* be consulted under s. 9 of the Act, as he or she will still be concerned with the physical wellbeing of the patient. This means that *both* doctors must be consulted — one under s. 7A and one under s. 9. Answers A and D are incorrect, as the question referred to who could take a sample under s. 7A.

Section 7A(2)(b) states that the request must be made to a police medical practitioner *unless* this is not reasonably practicable, in which case the request may be made to any other medical practitioner (*other than the one clinically responsible for the patient*). Answer C is therefore incorrect.

The Road Traffic Act has been altered to enable registered health care professionals to take a sample of blood under s. 8 of the Act (station procedure), but not to take samples at a hospital, therefore answer D is incorrect.

Road Traffic, para. 3.5.10

Answer 5.34

Answer **B** — A specimen of blood may be taken under s. 9 of the Road Traffic Act 1988, from a patient at a hospital, provided the doctor in immediate charge of his or her case agrees. Section 9 applies to both breath samples and samples of blood.

However, if a patient provides a positive reading or fails to provide a sample at a hospital, he or she cannot be arrested while still a 'patient' (s. 6(5)). Answer B is therefore correct and answer C is incorrect as, even though the officer sought permission to take the second sample, the arrest that preceded it was unlawful.

Since the arrest was unlawful, answer A is incorrect, as the patient should not have been taken to a police station in these circumstances. However, if the person had been arrested *after* ceasing to be a patient, she could have been taken to the station to provide a sample (see *Webber* v *DPP* [1998] RTR 111).

Answer D is incorrect as permission must be sought from a doctor for *each* sample that is required under s. 9(1).

Road Traffic, para. 3.5.10

6 | Insurance

STUDY PREPARATION

Insurance matters are straightforward and, after the detail of the previous chapter, are also relatively brief.

It is important to understand the requirements for compulsory insurance and the main related offences — including causing and permitting.

The duties on drivers and owners in relation to production of insurance documents are also important when studying this area.

QUESTIONS

Question 6.1

NEWBURY persuaded DAVIS to lend him his car to take his mother shopping. DAVIS agreed to do so, but on condition that NEWBURY arranged his own insurance. While driving DAVIS's car, NEWBURY was involved in an accident, and it was discovered that he had no insurance and that DAVIS's insurance did not cover him to drive either.

Would DAVIS be guilty of 'permitting' an offence by NEWBURY of driving without insurance?

A Yes, because permitting without insurance is an offence of absolute liability.
B No, because he told NEWBURY to insure the car before driving it, and has therefore discharged any liability for this offence.
C Yes, because even though he told NEWBURY to insure the car, he should have seen evidence that he had done so.
D No, because permitting without insurance is not an offence of absolute liability.

83

6. Insurance

Question 6.2

DOUGLAS was stopped while driving GARCIA's motor vehicle on a road. He was asked to produce his driving documents, including his insurance certificate. It transpired that GARCIA's certificate of insurance had expired, and DOUGLAS did not have a policy of his own to cover his use of the vehicle. DOUGLAS claimed that he was employed by GARCIA and that he was using the vehicle in the course of employment.

If both persons were to be prosecuted, with whom does the burden of proof lie, in relation to DOUGLAS' claim to be employed by GARCIA?
A   In relation to both persons, the prosecution.
B   In relation to DOUGLAS, the defence; in relation to GARCIA, the prosecution.
C   In relation to DOUGLAS, the prosecution; in relation to GARCIA, the defence.
D   In relation to both persons, the defence.

Question 6.3

BROWN was involved in a road traffic collision while driving his employer's delivery van in the course of his work. The collision occurred about two miles from his normal delivery route. At the time, BROWN was helping a friend by giving him a lift. The insurance policy for the van allows its use in connection with business only and it is company policy not to carry passengers in vehicles. BROWN does not have an insurance policy of his own and the journey was not authorised by his company.

Would the insurance policy for the van cover BROWN's use of the vehicle at the time of the collision?
A   Yes, BROWN's use of the vehicle would be covered in these circumstances.
B   No, because the van was being used in a manner not authorised by BROWN'S employer.
C   No, as BROWN has made a detour from his normal route, his use of the vehicle would not be covered.
D   No, as the van was not being used for business purposes at the time.

Question 6.4

GRIFFITHS owned a small van, which was insured for social, domestic and pleasure purposes only. His friend, LONGMAN, was moving house and GRIFFITHS helped him by moving furniture in the van, to LONGMAN's new house. Because this entailed several trips, LONGMAN reimbursed GRIFFITHS' petrol costs.

6. Insurance

Would GRIFFITHS be covered by his insurance policy for the use of the van in these circumstances?

A No, the use of the van would amount to a business arrangement, regardless of whether money was paid to GRIFFITHS.
B No, because money was paid to GRIFFITHS and the van was being used for purposes other than social, domestic or pleasure.
C No, either because money was paid to GRIFFITHS, or because the van was being used for purposes other than social, domestic or pleasure.
D Yes, this will not amount to a business arrangement, regardless of whether payment was paid to GRIFFITHS.

Question 6.5

Under s. 144 of the Road Traffic Act 1988, certain vehicles are exempt from the requirement for insurance.

Which of the following vehicles are **not** covered by the exemption?
1. A vehicle owned by the National Criminal Intelligence Service.
2. A motor vehicle being towed by another vehicle.
3. A vehicle owned by an off-duty police officer being used for police purposes.

A Vehicle 2 only.
B Vehicles 1 and 3 only.
C All of the above.
D Vehicles 2 and 3 only.

Question 6.6

Section 165 of the Road Traffic Act 1988 provides the authority for a constable to require the production of a certificate of insurance from the driver of a motor vehicle on a road or public place.

Following such a requirement, who may produce the certificate?

A Only the person who was driving the vehicle at the time the requirement was made.
B Only the person who was the owner of the vehicle at the time the requirement was made.
C Any person nominated by the person of whom the request is made.
D Any person nominated by the person of whom the request is made, provided they were nominated at the time the request was made.

6. Insurance

Question 6.7

STINTON had broken his arm and asked his friend FLEMING to drive him to the pub. On their way there, FLEMING was involved in an accident, and STINTON further damaged his broken arm. It was discovered that FLEMING was not insured to drive the vehicle. STINTON had to give up work because of the long-term damage to his arm, and made a claim for compensation to the Motor Insurers' Bureau (MIB) for damages.

Is STINTON's claim likely to succeed in these circumstances?

A No, as passengers in the offending vehicle are not entitled to claim.
B Yes, as he was not involved in a criminal act at the time of the accident.
C No, as he was a passenger who was *using* the vehicle at the time.
D Yes, as the driver of the vehicle is known and was uninsured.

Question 6.8

HOLDING was travelling as a passenger in his son's car. HOLDING's son was involved in a road traffic collision, when he collided with a stationary car. As a result, HOLDING sustained spinal injuries, which meant that he had to give up work. It was later discovered that HOLDING's son had no insurance for his car, therefore HOLDING made a claim to the Motor Insurers' Bureau (MIB), for damages as a result of the accident.

In which of the circumstances below could the MIB deny liability for the injuries caused to HOLDING?

A If it could be shown that he either knew or ought to have known that his son was not insured.
B Only if it could be shown that he actually knew that his son was not insured.
C Because HOLDING himself was not responsible for the collision, the claim cannot be refused.
D Because HOLDING's son was not involved in a criminal act, the claim cannot be refused.

6. Insurance

ANSWERS

Answer 6.1

Answer **B** — Permitting the use of a vehicle by another without insurance is an offence under s. 143 of the Road Traffic Act 1988, and generally the offence is one of absolute liability. Answer D is therefore incorrect.

If, however, a person allows another to use his or her vehicle on the express condition that the other person insures it first, the lender cannot be guilty of 'permitting' (*Newbury v Davis* [1974] RTR 367). There is no mention of having to check the person's certificate before allowing him or her to drive, and presumably stating the condition will suffice. Answers A and C are therefore incorrect.

Road Traffic, para. 3.6.2.1

Answer 6.2

Answer **B** — Section 143(3) of the Road Traffic Act 1988 provides a statutory defence for an employee, if he or she is using the employer's vehicle without insurance, provided he or she was not the owner of the vehicle, it was used in the course of his or her employment and he or she did not know or have any reason to believe that the vehicle was not insured. The burden of proof lies with the *employee* and the issue will be judged on the balance of probabilities (*R v Carr-Briant* [1943] All ER 156). Answers A and C are therefore incorrect.

Where an *owner* is suspected of committing an offence of using, causing or permitting the use of a motor vehicle on a road without insurance, the burden of proof lies with the *prosecution* to show the driver was acting in the course of his or her employment. The driver's statement that he or she was doing so will not in itself be sufficient to convict the owner of the offence of using (*Jones v DPP* [1999] RTR 1). Answers C and D are therefore incorrect.

Road Traffic, paras 3.6.2, 3.6.2.2

Answer 6.3

Answer **A** — A vehicle may be insured for business purposes, and normally, if an employee deviates from the ordinary course of his or her duties, the policy will be invalidated. However, it was decided in the case of *Ballance v Brown* [1955] Crim LR 384 that taking a two-mile detour to give someone a lift will not necessarily invalidate the employer's insurance. Answers C and D are therefore incorrect. In a further case that

6. Insurance

emphasises this point, *Marsh* v *Moores* [1949] 2 All ER 27, it was held that an employee driving an employer's vehicle in an unauthorised manner will not negate the effect of the insurance policy. Answer B is therefore incorrect.

Road Traffic, para. 3.6.2.3

Answer 6.4

Answer **D** — Lending a vehicle to a friend in return for payment reimbursing petrol costs has been held *not* to contravene s. 143 of the Road Traffic Act 1988, even when the vehicle was insured only for social, domestic and pleasure purposes (see *Lee* v *Poole* [1954] Crim LR 942). Answers B and C are incorrect for this reason. In the same case, it was held that using the vehicle to help a friend to move house will still amount to using the vehicle for social, domestic and pleasure purposes, therefore answer A is also incorrect.

Road Traffic, para. 3.6.2.3

Answer 6.5

Answer **A** — Statements 1 and 3 are incorrect. Among the vehicles listed as **exempt** from requiring insurance are:

- crown vehicles, while being used as such (see the Scottish case of *Salt* v *MacKnight* 1947 SC (J) 99);
- police authority vehicles and vehicles being used for police purposes — which includes a vehicle owned by an off-duty police officer being used for police purposes (*Jones* v *Chief Constable of Bedfordshire* [1987] RTR 332); *and*
- a vehicle owned by the National Criminal Intelligence Service or the National Crime Squad (s. 144(2)(ba) of the Road Traffic Act 1988).

Statement 2 is incorrect. A motor vehicle being towed by another vehicle will still be a 'motor vehicle', which means that it will still require insurance when used on a road (*Milstead* v *Sexton* [1964] Crim LR 474).

Consequently, answers B, C and D are incorrect.

Road Traffic, para. 3.6.2.5

Answer 6.6

Answer **C** — The certificate need not be produced in person, which means that the person who was driving the vehicle may elect another person to produce it for him or her. Answer A is therefore incorrect.

6. Insurance

It is *not* necessary to 'nominate' the person at the time the request is made to produce the documents. Answer D is therefore incorrect.

Answer B is incorrect as the driver may at times be different from the owner; therefore the power exists in relation to the driver (unless of course the owner is suspected of using, causing or permitting, in which case he or she may be asked to produce under s. 165(1)(c) of the Road Traffic Act 1988).

Road Traffic, para. 3.6.2.6

Answer 6.7

Answer **C** — The purpose of the Motor Insurers' Bureau (MIB) is to provide compensation where someone is unable to pursue a valid claim against another following a road traffic accident, i.e. because the other party is not insured, not known or traceable, or insured by a company now in liquidation.

Where a person other than the driver is injured, it will be a road traffic accident. Such a person may make a claim (provided he or she does not fall within the categories listed below). Answer A is therefore incorrect.

The MIB will not compensate those who are involved in deliberate criminal acts, nor will it pursue a claim on behalf of a person who was 'using' a vehicle at a time he or she was a passenger. As the owner of the vehicle in the scenario was in it, and it was being used for his purpose, he was 'using' it without insurance and therefore cannot make a claim. Answers B and D are therefore incorrect.

Road Traffic, para. 3.6.3

Answer 6.8

Answer **A** — The Motor Insurers' Bureau (MIB) will generally deny liability for any damages or loss to passengers who *either* knew *or* ought to have known that the driver was uninsured (see *Akers* v *Motor Insurance Bureau* [2003] Lloyds Rep IR 427). Answer B is incorrect, as the claim *could* fail if the MIB thought the passenger ought to have known that his son was uninsured. This would be the case whether or not the passenger was not responsible for the collision, therefore answer C is incorrect. Also, it is irrelevant in this particular case that the driver was not involved in a criminal act. This may be a reason for refusing a claim in some circumstances, but the claim in the scenario could be refused for the reasons listed above. Answer D is therefore incorrect.

Road Traffic, para. 3.6.3

7 Safety Measures

> **STUDY PREPARATION**
>
> Safety measures cover a range of statutory provisions, including the requirements for seat belts, crash helmets and speed restrictions.
>
> Once again this is a pretty straightforward area.

QUESTIONS

Question 7.1

CLEMENT was driving on a road in his car and his daughter JUDY, aged 14, was in the rear of the car and was not wearing a seat belt, even though seat belts were fitted to the vehicle. CLEMENT was wearing a seat belt himself; however, he was stopped by Constable BRIERS who saw that JUDY was not wearing hers.

    Which person, if either, would commit an offence under the Road Traffic Act 1988, because of JUDY's failure to wear a seat belt?

- **A** JUDY only, because of her age.
- **B** Both CLEMENT and JUDY, because of JUDY's age.
- **C** Neither person, as JUDY was in the rear of the car.
- **D** CLEMENT only, because of JUDY's age.

Question 7.2

Section 14(4) of the Road Traffic Act 1988 allows a constable to demand the production of a medical certificate from a driver claiming exemption from having to wear a seat belt, while driving a motor vehicle on a road.

7. Safety Measures

Within what time period should such a certificate be produced?

A It must be produced on request, or within 7 days at a police station.
B It must be produced on request, or within 14 days at a police station.
C The driver must have it with him or her, to be produced on request immediately.
D It must be produced on request, or within 21 days at a police station.

Question 7.3

HARRISON was driving on a road in his car and his son JONATHAN, aged 9, was in the rear of the car. HARRISON was wearing a seat belt, but JONATHAN was not. The car was old, and was not fitted with seat belts to the rear. The front passenger seat was occupied by HARRISON's other son BARRY, aged 16. BARRY was wearing a seat belt.

Has HARRISON committed an offence in relation to JONATHAN's failure to wear a seat belt?

A Yes, because of JONATHAN's age.
B No, because seat belts were not fitted to the rear of the vehicle.
C Possibly, but it would depend on JONATHAN's height.
D Yes, he should have moved JONATHAN to the front seat.

Question 7.4

KRAUSER, aged 25, has a full licence to ride a motor cycle, and one day he gave his brother PAUL, aged 15, a ride on the road as a pillion passenger on the motor cycle. They were stopped by Constable FRY, because PAUL was not wearing a crash helmet. At the time, the motor cycle had a sidecar attached to it.

Who, if either, would commit an offence in these circumstances (because of PAUL's failure to wear a helmet)?

A Neither, as the motor cycle was fitted with a sidecar.
B Both, because of PAUL's age.
C KRAUSER only, because of PAUL's age.
D PAUL only, because of his age.

Question 7.5

Under the Transport Act 2000, certain roads may be designated as 'quiet lanes' or 'home zones'. Who is provided with the power to designate such roads?

A The local authority.
B The Secretary of State.

7. Safety Measures

C The local Chief of Police.
D The Highways Authority.

Question 7.6

HARVEY was driving in a car at 40 mph along a road, when he was stopped by Constable UNDERWOOD. The officer believed that HARVEY was speeding, as the road was a 'restricted road'.

What physical features must be apparent to the officer to identify the road as a 'restricted road'?

A Street lamps less than 200 yards apart and signs signifying the 30 mph speed limit.
B Street lamps not less than 200 yards apart or signs signifying the 30 mph speed limit.
C Street lamps not more than 200 yards apart or signs signifying the 30 mph speed limit.
D Street lamps not more than 200 metres apart or signs signifying the 30 mph speed limit.

Question 7.7

Which of the following statements, if any, is true in relation to 'temporary speed limits'?

A Where a driver contravenes a temporary speed restriction, corroboration is not required, but a notice of intended prosecution is.
B Where a driver contravenes a temporary speed restriction, both corroboration and a notice of intended prosecution are required.
C Where a driver contravenes a temporary speed restriction, corroboration is required, but a notice of intended prosecution is not.
D Where a driver contravenes a temporary speed restriction, neither corroboration nor a notice of intended prosecution is required.

Question 7.8

Constable WOODS and Constable HUSSEIN were on duty in a marked police vehicle. They were driving along a restricted road, which had a speed limit of 30 mph. They followed DICKSON, who was driving at 40 mph in his car, for about a mile. The officers stopped DICKSON and spoke to him.

Would the officers be able to give evidence of DICKSON's speed, in order to prosecute him for the offence of speeding?

A No, their evidence does not amount to corroboration, and would not be accepted in court.
B Yes, provided it can be shown that they saw the vehicle at exactly the same time.
C Yes, the evidence that they both saw the vehicle speeding is sufficient alone to prosecute.
D Yes, corroboration is not required, as the offence took place on a restricted road.

Question 7.9

In which of the following scenarios, if any, will an offence have been committed under the motorway regulations?
1. DUVALL rode a motor cycle with an engine/cylinder capacity of 99 cc on the motorway. He has passed his motorcycle test.
2. PASK held a full driving licence to drive a car, but was learning to drive a large goods vehicle. She drove the goods vehicle on the motorway.
3. FLETCHER was towing a caravan on the motorway and used the outside lane to overtake a vehicle.

A All of the above.
B Scenario 3 only.
C Scenarios 1 and 2 only.
D Scenarios 2 and 3 only.

7. Safety Measures

ANSWERS

Answer 7.1

Answer **A** — It is an offence under s. 14(3) of the Road Traffic Act 1988 to *drive* a motor vehicle, or *ride* in the *front* or *rear* of a motor vehicle while not wearing an adult seat belt. Since the offences can be committed in either the front or rear of the vehicle, answer C is incorrect. The offences can only be committed by people aged 14 and over. Section 14(3) of the Act states that *no person other than the person actually committing the contravention is guilty of an offence*. This means that the driver of the vehicle in the scenario would commit no offence under this Act (answers B and D are therefore incorrect). Since the person in the scenario had reached the age of 14, and therefore was responsible for her own actions, she would be the only person guilty of this particular offence.

Road Traffic, para. 3.7.2

Answer 7.2

Answer **A** — If a person holds a medical certificate signed by a doctor stating that the wearing of a seat belt by that person is inadvisable on medical grounds, that person will be exempt. If it is to be used in evidence in answer to a charge under s. 14(3) of the Act, the certificate must be produced to a constable on request, or within 7 days at a police station (s. 14(3)). Answers B, C and D are therefore incorrect.

Road Traffic, para. 3.7.2.1

Answer 7.3

Answer **B** — Under s. 15(3) of the Road Traffic Act 1988, a person must not drive a motor vehicle on a road when a child under 14 is in the rear of the vehicle and not wearing a seat belt. However, this offence is committed only when seat belts *are fitted* to the vehicle (which is not the case in this question).

A separate offence is committed under s. 15(3A), where a child under the age of 12 and under 150 cm in height is in the rear of the vehicle without wearing a seat belt. *However*, this offence is committed only when the front seat is fitted with a seat belt *and is unoccupied*. Since the front seat in the vehicle *was* occupied by the driver's other son, no offence will be committed, regardless of the age or height of the child (therefore answers A and C are incorrect). Further, if all the seats are occupied correctly,

7. Safety Meaures

there is no general requirement to move an adult out of a seat to give the child access to a seat belt, or to move a child from a back seat of a vehicle where there are no seat belts, to the front seat where there are. Answer D is therefore incorrect.

Road Traffic, para. 3.7.2.2

Answer 7.4

Answer **B** — Section 16(1) of the Road Traffic Act 1988 makes it an offence to ride on a motor cycle without a crash helmet. 'Ride on' includes being a pillion passenger.

If the pillion passenger is *under 16*, the offence is committed by *both the rider and the passenger*. If the pillion passenger is *16 or over*, he or she is responsible alone. This is in contrast to seat belt legislation, where young passengers *are not* responsible for their own actions. As the person in the question was 15, both he and the driver commit the offence. Answers C and D are therefore incorrect.

A motor cycle with a sidecar attached will still be a *motor bicycle* for the purposes of the section and the offence is committed. Answer A is therefore incorrect. If the passenger had been sitting in the sidecar, he *would* have been exempt from having to wear a crash helmet (s. 16(1)).

Road Traffic, para. 3.7.3.1

Answer 7.5

Answer **A** — Under the Transport Act 2000, certain roads may be designated as 'quiet lanes' or 'home zones' by *local authorities*. Consequently, answers B, C and D are incorrect.

Road Traffic, para. 3.7.4

Answer 7.6

Answer **C** — Under s. 82(1)(a) of the Road Traffic Regulation Act 1984, a 'restricted road' is one which has a system of street lamps *not more than 200 yards apart*. This is the minimum requirement, and these features will mean that 30 mph signs are not required (s. 85(5)). Answer A is therefore incorrect.

The street lamps must be *200 yards apart, or less*. Therefore, answers B and D are incorrect.

If a road does not have such street lamps, it must have traffic signs stating the speed limit (s. 85(4)). Conversely, a road with street lamps of less than 200 yards

7. Safety Measures

apart may have a higher speed limit than 30 mph, but there must be signs indicating the limit.

The speed limit for a 'restricted road' is 30 mph, and it is an offence to drive a motor vehicle on a road exceeding this limit (s. 81(1)).

Road Traffic, para. 3.7.4.1

Answer 7.7

Answer **D** — Section 88 of the Road Traffic Regulation Act 1984 deals with temporary speed limits. This section refers to speed *restrictions* and speed *limits*. Where a person contravenes a temporary speed restriction, corroboration is *not* required. A notice of intended prosecution is also *not* required. Answers A, B and C are therefore incorrect.

Road Traffic, para. 3.7.4.3

Answer 7.8

Answer **B** — Under s. 89(2) of the Road Traffic Regulation Act 1984, a person may not be convicted solely on the evidence of one person for exceeding the speed limit. In other words, corroboration is required (unless the offence took place on a motorway). Corroboration is required when the offence takes place on a restricted road. Answer D is therefore incorrect.

Corroboration is normally provided by equipment in a police vehicle; however, two police officers *may* provide sufficient evidence in a case of speeding, but the court will decide how much weight to give to such evidence. It is important to show that the officers saw the vehicle at *exactly* the same time (*Brighty v Pearson* [1938] 4 All ER 127). Answers A and C are incorrect for this reason.

Road Traffic, para. 3.7.4.6

Answer 7.9

Answer **B** — The Motorways Traffic (England and Wales) Regulations 1982 (SI 1982 No. 1163) stipulate which vehicles may use the motorways, and *how* they may be used:

- A motor cycle with an engine/cylinder capacity of less than *50 cc* is not allowed on the motorway.

- A learner driver may not use the motorway. However, a person who holds an ordinary licence may drive a LGV or a PCV and may do so on the motorway even if he or she is learning to drive those particular classes of vehicles.
- Regulation 12 lists vehicles which are prohibited from using the outside lane of a motorway. Vehicles drawing trailers are listed; a caravan is a trailer. Also listed are LGVs exceeding 7.5 tonnes and PCVs over 12 m long.

Consequently, an offence has been committed under scenario 3 only, and therefore answers A, C and D are incorrect.

Road Traffic, para. 3.7.5

8 | Other Measures Affecting Safety

STUDY PREPARATION

The areas covered by this chapter are wide and varied, ranging from the disposal of abandoned vehicles to powers under the Terrorism Act 2000.

Many of the police powers covered are particularly useful in practical situations and therefore will be of interest to those who train and test police officers.

QUESTIONS

Question 8.1

MILLS placed a handcart in a busy shopping precinct, in order to sell Christmas decorations. The stall was situated in a street, which was open to pedestrians only and where no vehicles were allowed. Constable CHADD was passing and asked MILLS to remove the handcart, as she believed it was causing an obstruction.

Under what circumstances, if at all, may Constable CHADD arrest MILLS for obstruction?

A None, as MILLS was not in charge of a motor vehicle or trailer.
B Only if MILLS refuses to remove the obstruction on request.
C None, as MILLS is not obstructing a road.
D Only if the general arrest conditions under s. 25 of the Police and Criminal Evidence Act 1984 are satisfied.

Question 8.2

The Terrorism Act 2000 provides the police with powers to place restrictions on parking, to prevent acts of terrorism.

In relation to this power, who may authorise such restrictions, and for how long?
- **A** A superintendent, for a period not exceeding 28 days.
- **B** An assistant chief constable/commander, for a period not exceeding 21 days.
- **C** An assistant chief constable/commander, for a period not exceeding 28 days.
- **D** A chief officer of police/commander, for a period not exceeding 28 days.

Question 8.3

Constable RYAN was working in uniform as part of a team preparing for a Royal visit in a city centre. An order was in place under the Terrorism Act 2000 to regulate parking along the route the Royal cortege intended taking, to prevent acts of terrorism. Constable RYAN came across a van parked outside a shop which was situated on the route and when she found the owner, she asked him to remove the vehicle before the cortege was due to arrive in two hours. Constable RYAN returned to the location an hour later and the vehicle was still parked outside the shop.

What power, if any, does Constable RYAN have to arrest the driver of the vehicle, under s. 51(3) of the Terrorism Act 2000, in these circumstances?
- **A** None, the driver commits no offence, as he has merely failed to remove the vehicle; he has not refused to do so.
- **B** Arrest the driver for failing to remove the vehicle when requested.
- **C** Arrest the driver for failing to remove the vehicle, provided he was given the proper warning.
- **D** None, the driver may only be reported for failing to remove the vehicle when requested.

Question 8.4

PAINES lives on a main road, on a sharp bend. PAINES owns a caravan, which he keeps on his drive. He returned from holiday one evening and went to bed, forgetting to place blocks under the caravan's wheels to prevent it from moving. During the night, PAINES' caravan rolled down the drive and into the middle of the road, causing a danger to passing motorists.

Has PAINES committed an offence under s. 22A of the Road Traffic Act 1988 (causing danger to other road users)?

8. Other Measures Affecting Safety

A No, as he did not intend to create a danger for road users.
B Yes, as he was reckless as to whether danger would be caused to road users.
C No, the offence may be committed only when a person interferes with equipment in the road.
D No, provided no injury or damage was caused by the caravan's presence.

Question 8.5

GRANT bought some fireworks, and one evening he discharged some rockets while standing on the pavement outside his house.

Has GRANT committed an offence by discharging the fireworks in these circumstances?

A No, as the fireworks were not discharged in the road.
B Yes, provided a danger was caused to people using the road.
C Yes, provided people using the road were injured, interrupted *or* endangered.
D Yes, the offence is committed by simply discharging the firework.

Note: This does not take account of s. 28 of the Town Police Clauses Act 1847 (wantonly discharge firework).

Question 8.6

AHMED used a 3.5 tonne van to deliver furniture. AHMED was delivering to a house situated in a street, which had a grass verge in the centre of the road dividing two carriageways. There were no parking spaces outside the delivery address; therefore, AHMED parked the vehicle on the grass verge until a space became available.

Has AHMED committed an offence contrary to s. 19 of the Road Traffic Act 1988, (parking commercial vehicles on verges)?

A No, because of the vehicle's weight.
B Yes, as the vehicle was parked on land in the centre of the road.
C Yes, provided the vehicle was causing a danger.
D No, as the vehicle was not parked on a verge at the side of a road.

Question 8.7

Section 22 of the Road Traffic Act 1988 provides an offence of leaving a vehicle in a position, or condition, or in circumstances as to involve danger of injury.

8. Other Measures Affecting Safety

In relation to when an offence may be committed under this section, which of the following statements is correct?

A It may be committed by a vehicle or a trailer, but only when stationary.
B It may be committed by a vehicle only, when stationary.
C It may be committed by a vehicle or trailer, when stationary or moving.
D It may be committed by a vehicle only, when stationary or moving.

Question 8.8

Which of the following statements, if either, is/are correct in relation to the issue of badges, under the Chronically Sick and Disabled Persons Act 1970?

1. The scheme applies only to offences under the Road Traffic Regulation Act 1984.
2. A local authority may require the return of a badge, where a person has misused it in a way which has led to at least two convictions.

A Statement 1 only.
B Statement 2 only.
C Both statements.
D Neither statement.

Question 8.9

HARRIS was in a multi-storey car park attached to a shopping centre. The car park was operated by a private company, which owned the shopping centre, but was open to the general public at the time. The car park was covered by CCTV and the night security guard saw HARRIS climb onto the bonnet of a car and then run over the roof, jumping off the vehicle from the boot. He did this to several vehicles in the car park. The night security guard called the police and when they arrived, HARRIS was walking away from the car park.

Has HARRIS committed the offence of tampering with vehicles, under s. 25 of the Road Traffic Act 1988, in these circumstances?

A No, because the vehicles were not on a road.
B No, because the car park was not owned by the local authority.
C Yes, because the vehicles were in a public place.
D No, because he did not interfere with the brake or mechanism of the vehicles.

8. Other Measures Affecting Safety

Question 8.10

Under s. 26(1) of the Road Traffic Act 1988, an offence is committed by a person who gets onto a vehicle while it is in motion, for the purpose of being carried.

Where may such an offence be committed, and in relation to which type of vehicle?

A Motor vehicle or trailer on a road or public place.
B Motor vehicle, on a road.
C Motor vehicle or trailer on a road.
D Mechanically propelled vehicle or trailer on a road.

Question 8.11

DOUGLAS lived near some woodland, which was accessible from the road. One day, he drove to the woodland in his van and abandoned a settee and two chairs in a clearing in the woods.

Has DOUGLAS committed an offence under the Refuse Disposal (Amenity) Act 1978 (disposing property on land)?

A No, the offence relates to abandoning a motor vehicle only.
B Yes, he has committed an offence in these circumstances.
C No, he has not abandoned anything on a highway or land forming part of a highway.
D No, the offence relates to abandoning a motor vehicle or part of a motor vehicle only.

Question 8.12

A cycle race was due to take place in a town centre on a Sunday. CAREY had parked a caravan on the road the night before, intending to sell burgers from it to spectators the next day. CAREY had left the caravan on double yellow lines and it was in a street which formed part of the route for the race. Constable SHEEHY was sent to the scene to arrange for its removal before the start of the race.

Did Constable SHEEHY have the authority to remove the vehicle in these circumstances?

A Yes, she had the authority to remove the vehicle herself or arrange its removal.
B No, she would have to arrange for CAREY to remove it.
C No, the vehicle was not causing an actual obstruction to people using the road.
D No, the power to remove vehicles applies to motor vehicles only.

8. Other Measures Affecting Safety

Question 8.13

PETERS owned a trials motor cycle, which was not intended for use on roads. Near PETERS' house is an area of common land and he took his motor cycle there one day. PETERS had just started up his motor cycle and had ridden onto the land, approximately 10 yards from the road, when he was stopped by Constable MENDEZ.

Has PETERS committed an offence of driving on land other than a road, in these circumstances?

A No, as he was not driving a motor vehicle.
B Yes, as he has driven on common land other than a road.
C No, he has driven within 15 yards of the road.
D Yes, as he has driven on common land within 15 yards of the road.

Question 8.14

SHAH has hired PRICE to do some building work at his house. PRICE has hired a skip from BARRY for a period of three weeks. After a week, neighbours complain to the police that the skip is unlit during the night and is causing a danger to motorists.

Who has committed an offence in relation to the skip in these circumstances?

A SHAH only.
B PRICE only.
C PRICE and BARRY only.
D BARRY only.

Question 8.15

KAHL was approaching a zebra crossing on his motor cycle when GIBBONEY stepped on to the crossing at the last moment. KAHL did not see GIBBONEY and drove over the crossing, nearly hitting him. GIBBONEY took down the registration number of KAHL's motor cycle.

In relation to KAHL's failure to stop at the pedestrian crossing, which of the following statements is true?

A He is guilty of driving without due care and attention in these circumstances alone, which is an absolute offence.
B He is guilty of failing to stop at the crossing and driving without due care and attention.

103

8. Other Measures Affecting Safety

C He is guilty of failing to stop at the crossing in these circumstances alone, which is an absolute offence.
D He is guilty of driving without due care and attention in these circumstances alone.

Question 8.16

TROTT was working as a school crossing patrol outside a school at 7.50 am. BOYCE was riding on the road on his pedal cycle, when TROTT stood in the road to allow some people to cross. As none of the people were school children, BOYCE did not stop his cycle. TROTT was wearing her uniform and exhibiting her sign at the time of the incident.

Has BOYCE committed an offence in these circumstances?
A No, because of the time of day.
B Yes, an offence has been committed.
C No, because the people crossing were not children.
D No, because he was not driving a motor vehicle.

8. Other Measures Affecting Safety

ANSWERS

Answer 8.1

Answer **D** — The offence may be committed under s. 137 of the Highways Act 1980 or reg. 103 of the Road Vehicles (Construction and Use) Regulations 1986 (SI 1986 No. 1078) or s. 28 of the Town Police Clauses Act 1847 (outside London). A power of arrest is provided for an offence committed under the Highways Act 1980 only, provided the general arrest conditions under s. 25 of the Police and Criminal Evidence Act 1984 are satisfied. Answer B is therefore incorrect.

The offence under the Highways Act 1980 requires a person to *wilfully obstruct the free passage along a highway*. There is no requirement that the person is using or in charge of a motor vehicle or trailer to commit an offence under this Act. Answer A is therefore incorrect.

A 'highway' is a way over which the public has a right to pass and re-pass by foot, horse or vehicle (*Lang* v *Hindhaugh* [1986] RTR 271). The offence may be committed on a highway under the Highways Act 1980. Answer C is therefore incorrect.

Road Traffic, paras 3.8.2, 3.1.3.11

Answer 8.2

Answer **C** — The power under the Terrorism Act 2000 is given to any officer of or above the rank of assistant chief constable/commander. Where it appears expedient to such a person to do so, he or she may authorise the imposition of prohibitions or restrictions on parking in a specified area for a period not exceeding 28 days. Answer C is therefore the only possible correct answer and answers A, B and D are incorrect.

Road Traffic, para. 3.8.2.1

Answer 8.3

Answer **D** — An order may be given under s. 48 of the Terrorism Act 2000 to impose parking restrictions where it appears expedient to do so to prevent acts of terrorism, by an officer above the rank of assistant chief constable commander. Any person parking in contravention of such an order commits an offence. An additional offence is committed by a person who permits a vehicle to remain at rest *or* fails to move such a vehicle, when ordered to do so by a constable in uniform (s. 51(3)) (refusal is not

8. Other Measures Affecting Safety

mentioned, therefore answer A is incorrect). A person will be guilty of a *summary offence* under s. 51(3). Since there is no power of arrest, answers B and C are incorrect (regardless of the type of warning given).

Road Traffic, para. 3.8.2.1

Answer 8.4

Answer **A** — The offence is committed under s. 22A of the Road Traffic Act 1988, when a person *intentionally and without lawful authority or reasonable excuse* causes anything to be on or over the road in such circumstances that it would be obvious to a reasonable person that to do so would be dangerous.

Although PAINES could be said to have been the cause of the danger, he did not intend the act to happen. The offence is *not* committed when a person is merely reckless. Answer B is therefore incorrect.

Under s. 22A the offender must intend to cause anything to be in a road, *or* intend to interfere with anything. The offence may be committed if either of those situations is present. There is no need to show that the person *intends* to create danger. Answer C is therefore incorrect.

There is no requirement to prove that a person was injured or property was damaged; it is the potential danger that matters. Answer D is therefore incorrect.

Road Traffic, para. 3.8.3

Answer 8.5

Answer **C** — Under s. 161 of the Highways Act 1980, a person commits an offence if he or she discharges any firearm or firework within 15.24 metres (50 feet) of the centre of the highway, and in consequence a user of the highway is injured, interrupted *or* endangered.

As the offence took place on the pavement, which would be 50 feet from the centre of the highway, answer A is incorrect.

Answer B is incorrect as a user of the highway must be injured, interrupted or endangered.

Answer D is incorrect as there must be a consequence, i.e. an injury, interruption or danger must occur as a result of the discharged firework.

Road Traffic, para. 3.8.3.1

8. Other Measures Affecting Safety

Answer 8.6

Answer **A** — Under s. 19 of the Road Traffic Act 1988, an offence is committed by a *heavy* commercial vehicle, which is parked wholly or in part on the verge of a road, or any land situated between two carriageways that is not a footway, or on a footway. Answer D is incorrect as the offence may be committed in the middle of the road also.

Answer B is incorrect as the vehicle was not a heavy commercial vehicle, i.e. one which exceeded 7.5 tonnes.

There is no requirement to prove that any danger was caused by the vehicle's presence. Answer C is therefore incorrect.

Road Traffic, para. 3.8.4.1

Answer 8.7

Answer **C** — An offence may be committed under s. 22 of the Road Traffic Act 1988 by a vehicle or a trailer drawn by it. Answers B and D are therefore incorrect.

The offence may be committed either by a stationary vehicle *or* by a moving vehicle, when the offence is connected with the conditions or circumstances (*Maguire* v *Crouch* (1940) 104 JP 445). Answer A is therefore incorrect.

Answer C is the only option which combines the answers correctly.

Road Traffic, para. 3.8.4.2

Answer 8.8

Answer **A** — Statement 1 is correct; the scheme will only apply to offences under the Road Traffic Regulation Act 1984.

Statement 2 is incorrect; a local authority may refuse to issue a badge, or require the return of a badge, where a person has misused it in a way which has led to at least *three* convictions.

Consequently, answers B, C and D are incorrect.

Road Traffic, para. 3.8.4.4

Answer 8.9

Answer **B** — An offence is committed under s. 25 of the Road Traffic Act 1988 when a person *gets onto a vehicle*, or tampers with the brake or mechanism of a vehicle. Since the offence may be committed in either of these circumstances, answer D is

107

8. Other Measures Affecting Safety

incorrect. Offences under this section may *only* be committed either on a road *or* in a car park owned by the local authority. The offence may not be committed in *any* public place, therefore answer C is incorrect. Since the offence is not restricted to vehicles parked on a road, answer A is also incorrect.

Road Traffic, para. 3.8.5

Answer 8.10

Answer **C** — An offence is committed under s. 26(1) of the Road Traffic Act 1988 when a person gets onto a motor vehicle *or* trailer while it is in motion *on a road*, for the purpose of being carried. Answer C is the only one containing the correct combination; therefore, answers A, B and D are incorrect.

Road Traffic, para. 3.8.5

Answer 8.11

Answer **B** — An offence may be committed under s. 2 of the Refuse Disposal (Amenity) Act 1978 either by abandoning a motor vehicle or anything which formed part of a motor vehicle (s. 2(1)(a)), or by abandoning any thing *other than a motor vehicle* (s. 2(1)(b)). Answers A and D are therefore incorrect.

The offence is complete when property, as referred to above, is abandoned *either* on any land forming part of the highway, *or* on any land in the open air. Presumably this would include private property, if it is in the open air. Answer C is therefore incorrect.

Road Traffic, para. 3.8.6

Answer 8.12

Answer **A** — Under the Removal and Disposal of Vehicles Regulations 1986 (SI 1986 No. 183), a constable may require the owner of a vehicle to remove it (reg. 3). To implement the removal of a vehicle under reg. 3, it must be broken down, causing a danger or obstruction, or committing an offence such as a parking offence.

Under reg. 4, a constable may remove a vehicle himself or herself, or arrange its removal. In these circumstances, a vehicle must have broken down, or have been abandoned without lawful authority.

In the circumstances of the question, the officer could arrange for the removal of the vehicle without contacting the owner, as the vehicle is on yellow lines without lawful authority. Answers B and C are therefore incorrect.

8. Other Measures Affecting Safety

The 1986 Regulations are not restricted to 'motor' vehicles, and therefore a caravan will be a trailer, which in turn will be a vehicle. Answer D is therefore incorrect.

Road Traffic, para. 3.8.6.2

Answer 8.13

Answer **B** — Under s. 34 of the Road Traffic Act 1988, a person commits an offence who drives a *mechanically propelled vehicle* on any common land, moorland or land of any other description, not being part of a road.

The offence has been reworded by the Countryside and Rights of Way Act 2000, which extended the offence to include 'mechanically propelled' vehicles, rather than 'motor vehicles'. Answer A is therefore incorrect.

As soon as the person drives on the land, he or she commits the offence. Answer D is therefore incorrect.

A defence is provided for a person who has driven onto the land within 15 yards of the road *in order to park the vehicle.* There is no general defence of driving within 15 yards of the road only. Answer C is therefore incorrect.

Road Traffic, para. 3.8.7

Answer 8.14

Answer **D** — Under s. 139(4)(a) of the Highways Act 1980, a skip which has been deposited on a road must be 'properly lighted' during the hours of darkness. Section 139(4) states that the *owner* of the skip will be responsible for ensuring that it complies with the conditions imposed under the Act. Answer A is therefore incorrect.

Section 139(11) of the Act states that if a skip is either hired, or made subject of a hire purchase agreement for *not less than one month*, the person in *possession* of it will become the 'owner'. Since the builder in the scenario hired it for three weeks, which *is* less than a month, the actual owner, BARRY, retains responsibility for it. Answers B and C are therefore incorrect.

Road Traffic, para. 3.8.8

Answer 8.15

Answer **C** — The failure by a driver to stop at a crossing in contravention of the Regulations made under the Road Traffic Regulation Act 1984 is an absolute offence. There is no need to show any particular state of mind by the driver. Further, the

8. Other Measures Affecting Safety

failure by a driver to observe the crossing Regulations will *not* in itself provide sufficient proof that a person has driven without due care and attention (*Gibbons* v *Kahl* [1956] 1QB 59). Further proof would be required, although such evidence may be presented as part of a case.

Consequently, answers A, B and D are incorrect.

Road Traffic, para. 3.8.9.5

Answer 8.16

Answer **B** — Section 28 of the Road Traffic Regulation Act 1984 has been amended by the Transport Act 2000. There are no longer restrictions as to the time of day that an offence may be committed (formerly the hours were 0800 hrs to 1730 hrs). Answer A is therefore incorrect.

A further effect of the 2000 Act was that school crossing patrols are no longer restricted to stopping vehicles for *children* to cross. They may stop vehicles to allow anyone to cross safely. Answer C is therefore incorrect.

The offence may be committed by a person who is driving or propelling a *vehicle*. There is no requirement for a person to be driving a motor vehicle. Answer D is therefore incorrect.

Road Traffic, para. 3.8.9.6

9 | Construction and Use

> **STUDY PREPARATION**
>
> The area of construction and use probably typifies what most police officers associate with road traffic legislation.
>
> Seen by many as pedantic 'train spotter' law dealing with minor mechanical issues, construction and use legislation is in reality of some practical significance to patrol officers and the wider remit of road safety.
>
> The level of detail that police officers and examination candidates are expected to know has been greatly reduced over recent years, but there is still quite a lot of factual information to absorb.
>
> Although you could probably fill a book such as this with construction and use questions, you will be relieved to find that only a selection of some more relevant points has been included in this chapter.

QUESTIONS

Question 9.1

Regulation 27 of the Road Vehicles (Construction and Use) Regulations 1986 sets out the requirement for the depth of tread required for tyres fitted to motor vehicles, which are used on the road.

What is the minimum depth of tread allowed on such tyres?
- **A** 1.6 mm throughout a continuous band across the whole of the tyre, and around the entire circumference.
- **B** 1 mm throughout a continuous band across the central 3/4 section of the tyre, and around the entire circumference.

9. Construction and Use

C 1 mm throughout a continuous band across the whole of the tyre, and around the entire circumference.

D 1.6 mm throughout a continuous band across the central 3/4 section of the tyre, and around the entire circumference.

Question 9.2

SMITHERS was reversing an agricultural tractor along road and at the time he was towing a trailer loaded with hay. He was involved in a road traffic collision when he reversed into a vehicle which was parked at the side of the road. Constable BANNER attended the scene, and when she examined the vehicles, she noticed that two of the tyres on the trailer were devoid of tread. SMITHERS was reported for these offences; however, he pleaded not guilty in court, claiming that the trailer was exempt from the Road Vehicles (Construction and Use) Regulations 1986, in relation to tyres.

Who would bear the burden of proof, in relation to SMITHERS' claim, that the vehicle was exempt?

A The onus would be on the defence to show that the vehicle was exempt.
B The onus would be on the prosecution to show that the vehicle was not exempt.
C The question is not relevant; a trailer is not an agricultural motor vehicle and is not exempt.
D The question is not relevant; this is an absolute offence, no vehicle is exempt from the Regulations.

Question 9.3

WATSON is a taxi driver. One evening, WATSON pulled up outside a customer's house and sounded the taxi's horn several times, to attract the person's attention. The customer lived in a built up area and WATSON's taxi was stationary. The time was 11.35 pm.

Has WATSON committed an offence under reg. 99 of the Road Vehicles (Construction and Use) Regulations 1986?

A Yes, because it was after 11.00 pm and the vehicle was stationary.
B No, because it was not before 11.30 pm.
C Yes, because the vehicle was stationary.
D No, because the vehicle was stationary.

9. Construction and Use

Question 9.4

WINSTON parked outside a newsagent's shop in his car. He was accompanied by BREEN, who was sitting in the front passenger seat. Before WINSTON entered the shop, he turned off the car engine, but forgot to set the handbrake. BREEN realised what had happened and pulled the handbrake up before WINSTON returned.

Has WINSTON committed the offence of 'quitting' in these circumstances?
A Yes, provided BREEN was not a full licence holder.
B No, as the engine was not left running.
C No, as BREEN was in a position to intervene.
D Yes, regardless of whether BREEN had a full licence.

Question 9.5

Section 40A of the Road Traffic Act 1988 deals with the use of a vehicle on a road, in a dangerous condition.

To which of the following does the term 'dangerous' apply?
A Motor vehicle only, together with the passengers carried in or on it, or its accessories and equipment.
B Motor vehicle or trailer, together with the passengers carried in or on it, or its accessories and equipment.
C Motor vehicle, together with the passengers carried in or on it, or trailer together with its accessories and equipment.
D Motor vehicle only, together with any accessories and equipment it is fitted with.

Question 9.6

Regulation 3 of the of the Road Vehicles (Construction and Use) Regulations 1986 sets out the definition of 'daytime hours' and 'hours of darkness', which are relevant to offences committed in relation to lights on vehicles.

Which of the below statements correctly reflects the definition under reg. 3 of the 1986 Regulations?
A Half hour after sunrise and half hour before sunset; half hour before sunset and half hour after sunrise.
B Half hour before sunrise and half hour before sunset; half hour before sunset and half hour before sunrise.

113

9. Construction and Use

C   Half hour before sunrise and half hour after sunset; half hour after sunset and half hour before sunrise.
D   Half hour after sunrise and half hour after sunset; half hour after sunset and half hour after sunrise.

Question 9.7

DOMINGUEZ was driving his car on a road through a built up area at 1.00 pm, when he was stopped by Constable HIND. The officer examined DOMINGUEZ's car and discovered that the rear nearside light was defective.

What general exemption, under the Road Vehicles Lighting Regulations 1989, may DOMINGUEZ claim, to avoid prosecution for the defective light?

A   None, as the exemption applies to headlamps only.
B   That the defect occurred during the journey, or arrangements have been made to rectify it as soon as possible.
C   That the defect occurred during the journey.
D   That the defect has only recently occurred, and arrangements have been made to rectify it.

Question 9.8

Which of the following statements, if either, is/are correct, in relation to the testing of vehicles under s. 47 of the Road Traffic Act, 1988?

A   Police vehicles must submit to a test one year after they are first used on a road.
B   Police vehicles must submit to a test three years after they are first used on a road.
C   Police vehicles must submit to a test three years after they are first manufactured.
D   Police vehicles need not submit to a test at all.

Question 9.9

SETHI took her car to JEROME's garage as the test certificate was due for renewal. When SETHI returned for her vehicle, JEROME told her that her car had passed, but repairs had been necessary to the brakes and steering. SETHI paid JEROME £200, but as she was driving home, the steering felt unsteady. She took the car to another garage, where she was told that it was unroadworthy and required further repairs.

9. Construction and Use

Would JEROME have committed an offence under s. 75 of the Road Traffic Act 1988 (supplying an unroadworthy vehicle), in these circumstances?

A No, as JEROME did not sell the vehicle to SETHI.
B Yes, the offence is complete in these circumstances.
C No, as SETHI is the owner of the vehicle, JEROME could not supply it to her.
D No, because SETHI had to pay JEROME for the repairs.

Question 9.10

CRAIG realised that the test certificate on his car had expired. His friend, WALSH, owned a garage and was authorised to issue MOT certificates. CRAIG drove his car to WALSH's garage, where it failed the MOT test. CRAIG made arrangements to return the car the next day for work to be carried out, in order to pass the test.

Has CRAIG committed an offence in relation to the vehicle in these circumstances, by driving it either to or from the garage?

A Yes, on his way there only, as he had not arranged a test for the vehicle in advance.
B Yes, on his way there and on his way home, as he had not arranged to test the vehicle in advance.
C No, as he was taking the vehicle to be tested, and returning it after it had been refused a certificate.
D Yes, on his way there only; he is exempt in relation to the return journey, as the vehicle had been refused a test certificate.

Question 9.11

Section 68 of the Road Traffic Act 1988 provides police officers with the power to direct goods vehicles and large passenger carrying vehicles to a place to be examined.

What restrictions are placed on officers exercising these powers?

A Any such vehicle may be directed to any suitable place as directed by the officer.
B Stationary vehicles may be directed to a suitable place within two miles of the location.
C Stationary vehicles may be directed to a suitable place within five miles of the location.
D Any such vehicle may be directed to a suitable place within five miles of the location.

9. Construction and Use

Question 9.12

Which of the following statements is/are correct in relation to the power under reg. 74 of the Road Vehicles (Construction and Use) Regulations 1986 to inspect vehicles on premises following a road traffic accident?
1. The power may be exercised by police officers in uniform only.
2. There is no power of entry provided by the regulation.
3. The inspection must take place within 24 hours of the accident.

A   Statements 1 and 2 only.
B   Statement 2 only.
C   Statements 2 and 3 only.
D   Statements 1 and 3 only.

9. Construction and Use

ANSWERS

Answer 9.1

Answer **D** — Regulation 27 of the Road Vehicles (Construction and Use) Regulations 1986 (SI 1986 No. 1078) sets out a number of specific defects that will make tyres unlawful. The Road Vehicles (Construction and Use) (Amendment) (No. 4) Regulations 1990 (SI 1990 No. 1981) increased the depth of tread requirement to 1.6 mm from 1 mm. Answers B and C are incorrect for this reason.

The depth of tread must be 1.6 mm throughout a continuous band across the *central 3/4 section of the tyre*, and around the entire circumference. Answer A is therefore incorrect. Answer C is also incorrect for this reason.

Road Traffic, para. 3.9.4.2

Answer 9.2

Answer **A** — Certain vehicles are exempt from the requirement to have tyres that conform to reg. 27 of the Road Vehicles (Construction and Use) Regulations 1986 (defective tyres). Answer D is incorrect, because these exemptions show that this is not an absolute offence. Amongst the vehicles which are exempt from the requirements are agricultural motor vehicles driven at not more than 20 mph and *agricultural trailers* being drawn at no more than 20 mph (therefore answer C is incorrect). The onus is on the *defendant* to show that the vehicle falls into an exempted category (answer B is incorrect).

Road Traffic, para. 3.9.4.2

Answer 9.3

Answer **C** — Under reg. 99 of the Road Vehicles (Construction and Use) Regulations 1986, a person commits an offence by using the audible warning instrument while the vehicle is stationary on the road *or* if it is used between 11.30 pm and 7.00 am. The offence is complete if one of these circumstances is met. Answer B is therefore incorrect.

Answer A is incorrect as the offence is committed after 11.30 pm, not 11.00 pm.

Answer D is incorrect; the offence was committed because the vehicle *was* stationary.

Road Traffic, para. 3.9.4.4

9. Construction and Use

Answer 9.4

Answer **A** — Regulation 107 of the Road Vehicles (Construction and Use) Regulations 1986 prohibits motorists from leaving a motor vehicle unattended on a road unless the engine has been stopped *and* the handbrake has been set (*Butterworth* v *Shorthouse* [1956] Crim LR 341). This means that the offence will be committed if the driver allows either of these circumstances to occur. Answer B is therefore incorrect.

A driver will not commit an offence if the vehicle is left 'attended'. For a person to be 'attending' a vehicle in these circumstances, he or she must be *licensed* to drive it *and* be in a position to intervene. Answers 108 C and D are incorrect; a person must be the holder of a full driving licence and be in a position to intervene.

Road Traffic, para. 3.9.4.5

Answer 9.5

Answer **B** — Section 40A of the Road Traffic Act 1988 deals with *either* a motor vehicle or a trailer, which is used in such a way that involves a danger of injury to any person. Answers A and D are therefore incorrect.

The offence may be committed in a number of ways, including the number of passengers carried in or on either of the above vehicles, or the manner in which they are carried; *or* the condition of the vehicle itself or of its accessories and equipment. Answer C is therefore incorrect.

The offence may also be committed if the vehicle presents a danger because of the purpose for which it is used.

Road Traffic, para. 3.9.4.10

Answer 9.6

Answer **C** — A vehicle fitted with obligatory lamps must keep them lit during the 'hours of darkness', (reg. 25 of the of the Road Vehicles (Construction and Use) Regulations 1986). Regulation 3 of the 1986 Regulations defines the 'daytime hours' and the 'hours of darkness' as: *half hour before sunrise and half hour after sunset*; and *half hour after sunset and half hour before sunrise*, respectively. Since answer C contains the only correct combination, answers A, B and D are incorrect.

Road Traffic, para. 3.9.5.2

9. Construction and Use

Answer 9.7

Answer **B** — It is an offence under reg. 23 of the Road Vehicles Lighting Regulations 1989 (SI 1989 No. 1796) to use, cause or permit to be used a vehicle on a road unless the relevant lamps are clean and in good working order.

There is, however, an exemption under reg. 23(3): if the vehicle is being used during daytime hours and the defect only happened during the journey, *or* if arrangements have been made to rectify it with all reasonable expedition. Answers C and D are therefore incorrect.

The exemption applies to all relevant lamps, not just headlamps. Answer A is therefore incorrect.

Road Traffic, para. 3.9.5.8

Answer 9.8

Answer **D** — Certain vehicles must be tested after one year. These include, motor vehicles having more than 8 seats, which are used to carry passengers, taxis, ambulances and large goods vehicles, but **not** police vehicles, which means answer A is incorrect. All other motor vehicles must be tested three years after they were first *used on the road*. Answer C is incorrect because of answer D, but it would be incorrect *whatever* vehicles were mentioned in the question.

Police vehicles and fire engines are *not* listed. In fact vehicles *provided* for police purposes are exempt from requiring a test certificate. Consequently, answers A, B and C are incorrect.

Road Traffic, para. 3.9.6

Answer 9.9

Answer **B** — It has been held that where a garage returned a vehicle to an owner, after stating that it had been repaired and had passed its MOT, when in fact it was unroadworthy, the garage committed the offence of supplying an unroadworthy vehicle (*Devon County Council* v *DB Cars* [2002] Crim LR 71). In this case, the court held that 'supplying' involved a transfer of physical control of an item from one person to another (answer D is incorrect). It is both immaterial that the owner had to pay for the repairs, and that the owner did not buy the vehicle from the offender, therefore answers A and C are incorrect.

Road Traffic, para. 3.9.6

9. Construction and Use

Answer 9.10

Answer **B** — There are exemptions to s. 47 of the Road Traffic Act 1988 (using a motor vehicle on a road without a test certificate), where a person is taking a vehicle to or from a testing station. However, a driver may only claim exemption if he or she is driving to *or from* a pre-arranged test. The key is whether the test was prearranged, and in this case it was not. Answer C is therefore incorrect.

Although they are worded differently, answers A and D are incorrect for the same reason. There is a further exemption for vehicles which have been refused test certificates. However, this exemption applies only when the vehicle is being driven, *by prior arrangement*, or brought from the relevant place where the work is being carried out. This exemption allows garage proprietors, who are not registered to supply test certificates, to take vehicles to and from testing stations, and again does not apply in these circumstances.

The last exemption, which again does not apply to the given facts, is where a vehicle is being towed to be broken up, following the refusal of a test certificate.

Road Traffic, para. 3.9.6

Answer 9.11

Answer **C** — The power conferred by s. 68 of the Road Traffic Act 1988 applies to *stationary* vehicles only. Answers A and D are therefore incorrect.

The section authorises a constable in uniform to direct a stationary vehicle to suitable premises, provided the place is no more than *five miles* from the location where the direction was made. Answers A, B and D are all incorrect for this reason.

Road Traffic, para. 3.9.6.2

Answer 9.12

Answer **B** — Statement 1 is incorrect. Although the power under reg. 74 of the Road Vehicles (Construction and Use) Regulations 1986 relates to 'reportable accidents', it may be exercised either by a police officer in uniform *or* by an authorised vehicle examiner.

Statement 2 is correct. There is no power of entry provided by this regulation.

Statement 3 is incorrect. The inspection must take place within *48* hours of the reportable accident.

Consequently, answers A, C and D are incorrect.

Road Traffic, para. 3.9.6.3

10 | Traffic Signs and Directions

Please note that the questions in this chapter relate to material in the Blackstone's Police Manuals which has been excluded from the OSPRE® syllabus for 2005.

> **STUDY PREPARATION**
>
> What can you say about traffic signs? There are mercifully few key principles and powers to learn here . . .

QUESTIONS

Question 10.1

A religious festival was taking place over a two-day period in a large park. The police placed cones on the road outside the park to prevent vehicles from parking outside and causing an obstruction. The officer in charge decided to leave the cones in place overnight, to restrict parking before the next day's event.

Did the officer in charge have the authority to leave the cones in place in between the two events?

A Yes, the officer may leave the cones in place for up to seven days from the time they were placed.

B No, the officer should have removed the cones following the potential obstruction and re-sited them before the next one.

C Yes, the officer may leave the cones in place for up to 36 hours from the time they were placed.

D No, the officer should have sought permission from the local traffic authority to maintain the cones in place following the original obstruction.

Question 10.2

Under reg. 15(1) of the Traffic Signs (Temporary Obstructions) Regulations 1997, certain people are authorised to place a 'keep right' sign at the scene of a

10. Traffic Signs and Directions

temporary obstruction by a breakdown vehicle, to warn other motorists of the obstruction.

Who is entitled to place such a sign, in order to warn of the obstruction?
A The person in charge of the vehicle only.
B The driver of the vehicle only.
C The person in charge of the vehicle, or a person accompanying it.
D An authorised person only.

Question 10.3

Section 163 of the Road Traffic Act 1988 deals with the power given to police officers in uniform to stop vehicles, when not engaged in the direction of traffic.

What restrictions are in place, in relation to the types of vehicles that may be stopped under this section?
A Mechanically propelled vehicles, or pedal cycles.
B Mechanically propelled vehicles only.
C Any vehicle.
D Motor vehicles only.

Question 10.4

Constable WALSH was on patrol in uniform in a marked police vehicle, when she attempted to stop a vehicle being driven by ASFI. The vehicle failed to stop and Constable WALSH lost sight of it a short while later. Constable WALSH conducted a PNC check and attended the registered owner, ASFI's, home address. The vehicle was parked around the corner. There was no reply at the address, but Constable WALSH had reason to believe that ASFI was inside the premises.

Did Constable WALSH have the power to enter the premises and arrest ASFI, in these circumstances?
A No, the offence is summary only.
B Yes, as this is an arrestable offence.
C No, as ASFI was not stopped while driving the vehicle.
D Yes, WALSH has the power to arrest for this offense and may enter the premises to do so.

10. Traffic Signs and Directions

Question 10.5

Who may exercise the power given under s. 35(1) of the Road Traffic Act 1988, to stop vehicles when engaged in the direction of traffic?

A A police officer in uniform, a traffic warden, or a community support officer.
B A police officer in uniform only.
C A police officer, whether in uniform or not, or a traffic warden.
D A police officer whether in uniform or not, or a community support officer.

Question 10.6

BECKER is a traffic warden who one day came across a road accident. BECKER began directing traffic until a police officer arrived. PETERS was walking along the pavement, which was blocked by one of the cars involved in the accident. BECKER asked PETERS to wait on the pavement until it was safe to walk in the road. PETERS refused to do so because he was in a hurry and walked out into the road, nearly causing another accident.

Did BECKER have the authority to demand PETERS' name and address in these circumstances?

A No, as this power is restricted to constables in uniform.
B No, as this power is restricted to constables.
C No, as a traffic warden's power is restricted to stopping vehicles.
D Yes, as PETERS failed to comply with the direction given to stop.

10. Traffic Signs and Directions

ANSWERS

Answer 10.1

Answer **A** — A traffic sign will include 'any object or device (whether fixed or portable) for conveying to traffic on roads . . . warnings, information, restrictions or prohibitions of any description' (s. 64 of the Road Traffic Regulation Act 1984).

Traffic signs may be placed by a constable or other person authorised by the chief officer of police in order, amongst other things, to prevent congestion or obstruction from traffic. The signs may remain in place for up to *seven* days (s. 67 of the 1984 Act). Answers B and C are therefore incorrect.

There is no requirement to seek permission from the local traffic authority. Answer D is therefore incorrect.

Road Traffic, para. 3.10.2

Answer 10.2

Answer **C** — Under reg. 15(1) of the Traffic Signs (Temporary Obstructions) Regulations 1997, the person in charge of the vehicle, *or* a person accompanying it is authorised to place a 'keep right' sign at the scene of a temporary obstruction by a breakdown or emergency vehicle, to warn other motorists of the obstruction. Answers A and B are therefore incorrect. The Regulations do not state that a person must be authorised, therefore, answer D is incorrect.

Road Traffic, para. 3.10.2.3

Answer 10.3

Answer **A** — The power to direct vehicles under s. 163(1) of the Act applies to *mechanically propelled vehicles* being driven on a road. Police officers are given a further power under s. 163(2), to stop *pedal cycles* being ridden on a road. Answer A is the only correct combination, which means that answers B, C and D are incorrect.

Road Traffic, para. 3.10.4.1

10. Traffic Signs and Directions

Answer 10.4

Answer **D** — Under s. 163(1) of the Road Traffic Act 1988, a person driving a mechanically propelled vehicle on a road must stop the vehicle on being required to do so by a constable in uniform. Since 1 October 2002, under s. 163(4), a constable in uniform may arrest a person without warrant if he or she has reasonable cause to suspect that the person *has* committed the offence. Answers A, B and C are incorrect. The power of entry under s. 17 of the Police and Criminal Evidence Act 1984 also applies to this offence; therefore answers A and C are incorrect.

Road Traffic, para. 3.10.4.1

Answer 10.5

Answer **C** — The power is *not* restricted to police officers in uniform, therefore answers A and B are incorrect. The power under s. 35 also applies to *traffic wardens*. Answer D is also incorrect.

Community Support Officers, who have been designated under sch. 4 to the Police Reform Act 2002, are given powers to stop vehicles within their relevant police area, but only for the purposes of carrying out road checks (see *Blackstone's General Police Duties*). Therefore, answers A and D are incorrect.

Road Traffic, para. 3.10.4.2

Answer 10.6

Answer **D** — A police officer in uniform engaged in the regulation of vehicular traffic in a road has the authority to stop pedestrians from proceeding (s. 37 of the Road Traffic Act 1988). This power is also given to traffic wardens (s. 96 of the 1988 Act). Answer C is therefore incorrect.

Under s. 169 of the Act, if a person fails to comply with a direction given under s. 37, a *constable* (not necessarily in uniform) has the authority to demand that person's name and address. Again, by virtue of s. 96 of the Act, this power is also given to traffic wardens. Answers A and B are therefore incorrect.

Road Traffic, para. 3.10.4.3

11 | Driver Licensing

Please note that the questions in this chapter relate to material in the Blackstone's Police Manuals which has been excluded from the OSPRE® Inspectors' Exam syllabus for 2005.

> **STUDY PREPARATION**
>
> The law relating to driver licensing is of considerable practical significance.
>
> You need to know how the licensing system works in terms of what licence is needed by what driver for what vehicle; you also need to know the relevant police powers in relation to licences and the attendant offences that can be committed.
>
> Of particular importance is the offence of disqualified driving and the provisions that apply to learner drivers and their supervisors.

QUESTIONS

Question 11.1

Section 87 of the Road Traffic Act 1988 makes it an offence for a person to drive a motor vehicle on a road otherwise than in accordance with a licence.

In relation to the burden of proof that the defendant was driving on a road and that he or she had a licence to do so, which of the following statements is correct?

- **A** The defence must prove that the defendant was not driving on a road, and that he or she had a licence to drive the vehicle.
- **B** The prosecution must show that the defendant was driving on a road; the defendant must show that he or she had a licence to do so.
- **C** This is an absolute offence; no further proof is required, other than the fact that the defendant was driving on a road.
- **D** The prosecution must show that the defendant was driving on a road and that he or she had did not have a licence to do so.

11. Driver Licensing

Question 11.2

What is the specified period of time allowed, before a person must renew a photocard driving licence?

A Every 10 years.
B Every 20 years.
C On a person's 70th birthday.
D Every 5 years.

Question 11.3

Section 164 of the Road Traffic Act 1988 provides a constable with the authority to demand the production of a driving licence from a person supervising the holder of a provisional driving licence.

Under what circumstances may a constable demand the production of a driving licence when such a person is no longer supervising a person who is driving a motor vehicle on a road?

A When he or she has reasonable cause to believe that the supervisor was committing an offence, or that the driver had been involved in an accident.
B Only when he or she has reasonable cause to believe that the driver was committing an offence.
C When he or she has reasonable cause to believe that the driver was committing an offence, or had been involved in an accident.
D When he or she has reasonable cause to believe that the person was supervising a driver who was driving a motor vehicle on a road.

Question 11.4

Constable HERSI was on duty when she stopped BELL, a learner driver, who was driving a motor vehicle on a road. BELL was accompanied by MARTIN, who was supervising him. Constable HERSI asked BELL and MARTIN to produce their driving licences. However, only MARTIN had his with him.

From whom could Constable HERSI require a date of birth in these circumstances?

A Either, but only if she suspects BELL has committed an offence.
B Either, but only if she suspects that MARTIN is under 18.
C From BELL, as MARTIN has produced a driving licence.
D From either, but only if she suspects that MARTIN is under 21.

127

11. Driver Licensing

Question 11.5

Section 101 of the Road Traffic Act 1988 sets out the minimum ages to enable a person to drive certain classes of vehicles.

In relation to this section, which of the following statements, if either, is/are correct?

1. A person must be at least 18 years of age in order to drive a medium-sized goods vehicle.
2. A person must be at least 16 years of age in order to drive a moped.

A   Statement 1 only.
B   Statement 2 only.
C   Both statements.
D   Neither statement.

Question 11.6

STACEY has recently left her husband KEITH and moved in with BEN. As a result, KEITH has refused to allow STACEY access to their children. She was the front seat passenger in BEN's car one day and BEN was driving, when they saw KEITH standing on the pavement waiting to cross the road. Because she was so upset by what had happened recently, STACEY persuaded BEN to drive straight at KEITH and knock him over. He did so, but fortunately KEITH sustained only minor injuries. They were both convicted of common assault at the magistrates' court, and the Crown Prosecution Service (CPS) asked the court to disqualify both defendants from driving.

Would the court be in a position to agree with the request made by the CPS in these circumstances?

A   Yes, a person may be disqualified on conviction for any offence.
B   Yes, but only in relation to BEN, as he was the driver.
C   No, as neither has been convicted of an offence under the Road Traffic Act 1988.
D   Yes, a person may be disqualified on conviction for common assault.

Question 11.7

Intelligence had been received that JANES, a disqualified driver, was driving to work regularly. Constable COOK was on patrol one morning, when he saw JANES leave his house and get into his car. Aware of the recent intelligence, Constable COOK approached the car and saw JANES place the keys in the ignition and try to start the car.

11. Driver Licensing

What power is available to Constable COOK to deal with JANES for the offence of disqualified driving, under s. 103 of the Road Traffic Act 1988, in these circumstances?

A Arrest JANES for attempting to drive while disqualified.
B He has no power to deal with JANES in these circumstances.
C Arrest JANES for disqualified driving, as he is about to drive the vehicle.
D Report for summons, as JANES is about to drive while disqualified.

Question 11.8

KLINE was driving a motor vehicle on a road, when he was stopped by Constable POPE. KLINE admitted that he was only 16 and did not possess a licence to drive the vehicle.

What power would Constable POPE have to arrest KLINE in these circumstances?

A None, KLINE should be reported for summons for driving other than in accordance with a licence.
B KLINE can be arrested for driving whilst disqualified in these circumstances.
C None, KLINE should be reported for summons for driving whilst disqualified.
D KLINE can be arrested for driving whilst disqualified by reason of his age.

Question 11.9

In relation to the proof required to prove an offence of driving while disqualified under s. 103 of the Road Traffic Act 1988, which of the following statements is correct?

A The prosecution will need to show the defendant was disqualified, and that he or she was aware of this fact.
B The prosecution will need to show the defendant was disqualified, but not that he or she was aware of this fact.
C The defendant will need to show that he or she was not disqualified, or that he or she was not aware of this fact.
D The offence is one of strict liability; the prosecution need only show that the defendant was driving a motor vehicle on a road.

Question 11.10

JELF was driving a motor vehicle on a road, when she was stopped by Constable STACEY. JELF admitted that she had been recently convicted of speeding, and had

129

11. Driver Licensing

been disqualified from driving until she passed a driving test. JELF was in possession of a provisional driving licence, but she was unaccompanied at the time she was stopped, and was not displaying 'L' plates.

What offence has JELF committed, and what power does Constable STACEY have to deal with her?

A Disqualified driving; report JELF for summons only.
B Failing to display 'L' plates and driving unaccompanied; report JELF for summons only.
C Driving other than in accordance with a licence; report JELF for summons only.
D Disqualified driving; JELF may be arrested.

Question 11.11

When a person completes a compulsory basic training course for provisional licence holders, riding motor bicycles and mopeds, he or she is issued with a certificate.

When does such a certificate expire?

A After one year.
B After two years.
C No time limit, certificates are valid until a test is passed.
D After three years.

Question 11.12

An instructor taking a basic training course for learner motor bicycles and mopeds is restricted as to how many people he or she may supervise at any one time.

How many people may an instructor supervise in these circumstances?

A Four.
B Two.
C Five.
D Three.

Question 11.13

POTTER was supervising GREEN, who was learning to drive. As they were travelling along the road, GREEN collided with a parked car. GREEN panicked and drove off after the accident, without stopping.

Does POTTER have a responsibility for GREEN'S actions in these circumstances?

11. Driver Licensing

A Yes, but only if he encouraged the actions.
B No, he is only there to supervise GREEN's driving.
C No, he is only there to provide tuition for GREEN.
D Yes, he should have ensured that GREEN remained at the scene.

Question 11.14

ARNOLD was acting as a supervisor to MAHMOOD, who was driving a motor vehicle on a road. ARNOLD had given MAHMOOD several lessons, but was not a registered driving instructor. MAHMOOD did not pay ARNOLD directly for the lessons, but gave him money each time to cover the cost of petrol.

Does ARNOLD need to be registered to give driving lessons in these circumstances?

A No, as he was not being paid directly for the lessons.
B No, as he did not have a commercial arrangement with MAHMOOD.
C Yes, as he had a commercial arrangement with MAHMOOD.
D No, any person may charge for giving driving lessons, if they have a full licence.

Question 11.15

Regulation 18 of the Motor Vehicles (Driving Licences) Regulations 1999 deals with new residents in the United Kingdom who hold a valid driving licence in their country of origin.

What do the Regulations state about the ability of such people to drive in the UK?

A They may drive for 12 months, but must obtain a provisional driving licence before driving on a road.
B They may drive for 12 months and may apply for a provisional driving licence during that time.
C They may not use their foreign driving licence, as they are a resident not a visitor.
D They may drive for 18 months and may apply for a provisional driving licence during that time.

Question 11.16

AMIR was involved in a road accident during the hours of darkness. A witness stated that AMIR had caused the accident by failing to comply with a 'Give Way' sign. AMIR

131

11. Driver Licensing

admitted to Constable WARE that he normally wore contact lenses, but had forgotten to wear them that night.

Under what conditions may Constable WARE require AMIR to submit to an eyesight test?

A   In daylight conditions, while wearing his contact lenses.
B   In darkness, without his contact lenses.
C   In darkness, while wearing his contact lenses.
D   In daylight conditions, without his contact lenses.

11. Driver Licensing

ANSWERS

Answer 11.1

Answer **B** — In proving the offence under s. 87 of the Road Traffic Act 1988, it is for the *prosecution* to show that the defendant was driving on a road. Answer A is therefore incorrect.

It is for the defendant to show that he or she had a licence to drive that class of vehicle (*John* v *Humphries* [1955] 1 All ER 793). In spite of this, it would be prudent for the prosecution to gather such evidence as is available to them, such as DVLA records. Answers C and D are therefore incorrect.

Road Traffic, para. 3.11.2

Answer 11.2

Answer **A** — The licence is renewable every 10 years, presumably because unfortunately, as we get older, our appearance changes! Answers B, C and D are therefore incorrect.

Road Traffic, para. 3.11.3.1

Answer 11.3

Answer **C** — Under s. 164 of the Road Traffic Act 1988, the power to demand production of a driving licence by a driver, or a person supervising the driver, of a motor vehicle on a road is restricted to the present tense only, where the driver is *not* suspected of *having committed an offence*, or *having been involved in an accident*. Therefore, if the officer simply has reasonable to cause to suspect a person *has* been driving a motor vehicle on a road, this would not provide sufficient authority to demand the production of a driving licence from either the supervisor or the driver. Answer D is therefore incorrect.

In order to demand production from a person who *has* been driving, the constable must have reasonable cause to believe that the *driver* (answer A is incorrect, as it refers to the supervisor) was either committing an offence *at that time*, or *had been* involved in an accident. Answer B is incorrect, as the constable may do so in either of these circumstances.

Road Traffic, para. 3.11.4.1

11. Driver Licensing

Answer 11.4

Answer **D** — The power to demand a person's date of birth in these circumstances is given by s. 164(2) of the Road Traffic Act 1988. If a person is driving a vehicle, and fails to produce a driving licence as requested, the officer may ask for his or her date of birth. There is no requirement to suspect that an offence has been committed. Answer A is therefore incorrect.

A constable may also demand a date of birth from a person who is supervising a driver, if he or she suspects that person to be under 21 years of age. Answer B is therefore incorrect. This power would also apply even if the person has produced a driving licence, provided the constable had reason to suspect that he or she is under 21. Answer C is therefore incorrect.

Road Traffic, para. 3.11.4.2

Answer 11.5

Answer **C** — A person will be disqualified from holding or obtaining a licence to drive a motor vehicle of a class specified in s. 101 of the Road Traffic Act 1988, if he or she is under the age specified for that class of vehicle.

Statement 1 is correct; the specified age for a medium-sized goods vehicle is 18. Statement 2 is also correct; the specified age for a moped is 16. Consequently, answers A, B and D are incorrect.

Road Traffic, para. 3.11.6

Answer 11.6

Answer **D** — The Powers of Criminal Courts (Sentencing) Act 2000 gives courts the power to disqualify any defendant from holding or obtaining a driving licence when convicting that person of any *criminal* offence. Similarly, where a court convicts a person of common assault or of any assault, or of aiding and abetting, counselling or procuring or inciting such an assault, the court may disqualify that person when the offence was committed by the use of a vehicle. Therefore, although STACEY was not actually driving the vehicle, she could still be disqualified by the court because of the joint nature of the offence and answer B is incorrect. Answer A is incorrect, as this power does not apply to *any* offence. Similarly, answer C is incorrect as the power may be applied even when the person has not been convicted of an offence under the Road Traffic Act 1988.

Road Traffic, para. 3.11.8

11. Driver Licensing

Answer 11.7

Answer **B** — Under s. 103 of the Road Traffic Act 1988, a person is guilty of an offence if, while disqualified for holding or obtaining a licence, he drives a motor vehicle on a road. The person must be *driving* to commit the offence, therefore answers C and D are incorrect.

The offence of driving while disqualified has now been made an arrestable offence; *however*, the offence is triable *summarily*. This means that there is no offence of attempting to commit the offence, and answer A is incorrect. The person in the question was not driving, as he was engaged in a preparatory act. Therefore he will not be guilty of an offence in these circumstances (which is why answer B is correct).

Recent case law has extended the meaning of 'driving' to include occasions where a person has been driving but has temporarily ceased (see *Shackleton* v *Chief Constable of Lancashire Police* [2001] EWCA Civ 1975, when a police officer saw a disqualified driver 'jogging' away from a car). Further guidance can be found in the case of *Pinner* v *Everett* [1969] 1 WLR 1266, when the House of Lords found that each case should be taken on its merits, but that a person could be driving if he or she:

- had actually stopped driving or intended carrying on (e.g. at a set of traffic lights);
- was still driving;
- had arrived at his or her destination or intended to continue to a further location;
- had been prevented or dissuaded from driving by someone else.

None of the above fit the circumstances in the question, as the person was about to start a fresh journey.

Road Traffic, para. 3.11.8

Answer 11.8

Answer **A** — Even though a person who drives a certain class of vehicle under age will be 'disqualified' from holding a licence, that person will not commit an offence of disqualified driving under s. 103 of the Road Traffic Act 1988. They will commit an offence of driving other than accordance with a licence, under s. 87(1) of the Act. Answers B, C and D are all incorrect for this reason.

The new power of arrest for disqualified driving (which is now an arrestable offence), will *not* apply in these circumstances; therefore, answers B and D are incorrect.

Road Traffic, para. 3.11.2

11. Driver Licensing

Answer 11.9

Answer **B** — The offence under s. 103 of the Road Traffic Act 1988 is one of strict liability. However, the prosecution will need to show more than just the fact that the defendant was driving a motor vehicle on a road. Answer D is therefore incorrect.

The prosecution *will* need to prove that the defendant was, in fact, a disqualified driver. As the onus is on the prosecution, answer C is incorrect.

However, there is no need for the prosecution to prove that the defendant knew of the disqualification (*Taylor* v *Kenyon* [1952] 2 All ER 726). Answer A is therefore incorrect.

Road Traffic, para. 3.11.8

Answer 11.10

Answer **D** — Where a person has been disqualified by the court until a test is passed, he or she has to comply with the requirements of a provisional licence holder. If a person fails to comply with these requirements, he or she commits the offence of *disqualified driving* (*Scott* v *Jelf* [1974] RTR 256). Answers B and C are therefore incorrect.

Disqualified driving is now an arrestable offence and the power will apply in these circumstances. Answer A is therefore incorrect.

Road Traffic, para. 3.11.8.1

Answer 11.11

Answer **B** — When a person completes a compulsory basic training course, he or she is issued with a certificate which is valid for two years, therefore answers A, C and D are incorrect.

Road Traffic, para. 3.11.9.1

Answer 11.12

Answer **D** — An instructor taking a training course for motor cycles and mopeds (compulsory basic training) may not supervise more than *three* provisional licence holders at one time. This is in contrast to an instructor taking a training course for 'large motor cycles' (direct access course). Here, the number of students an instructor can safely train is two. Answers A, B and C are therefore incorrect.

Road Traffic, para. 3.11.9.1

11. Driver Licensing

Answer 11.13

Answer **D** — A person supervising a learner driver is required not to provide tuition for the learner, but to 'supervise'. Answer C is therefore incorrect.

Supervising requires some positive action on behalf of the supervisor, and these duties extend to ensuring compliance with other legislative requirements, such as remaining at the scene of an accident (*Bentley* v *Mullen* [1986] RTR 7, or remaining sober when doing so (*DPP* v *Janman* [2004] EWHC 101). Answer B is therefore incorrect. There is no need to show encouragement to commit the offence, merely that the supervisor did not act to prevent the actions. Answer A is therefore incorrect.

Road Traffic, para. 3.11.9.5

Answer 11.14

Answer **C** — Any person may give driving lessons provided they do not charge money or money's worth in return. If a person wants to give driving lessons for payment, he or she must be registered in accordance with the provisions of Part V of the Road Traffic Act 1988. Answers A and D are therefore incorrect.

In the case of *Mahmood* v *Vehicle Inspectorate* (1998) 18 WRTLB 1, it was held by the Divisional Court that what mattered was that the instructor had some sort of arrangement with the learner driver and that the arrangement had a 'commercial flavour'. The fact that Arnold was receiving money's worth (a payment for petrol) may amount to a 'commercial flavour' for the purposes of this legislation. Answer B is therefore incorrect.

Road Traffic, para. 3.11.10

Answer 11.15

Answer **B** — Under reg. 18 of the Motor Vehicles (Driving Licences) Regulations 1999, visitors *and* new residents holding a valid driving licence from their country of origin may use that licence as a full licence to drive on the roads. Answer C is therefore incorrect.

Such drivers may drive for up to 12 months using their licence, and they may take a test during that period. Answer D is therefore incorrect. Drivers *may* apply for a provisional licence during the period, but this is not compulsory. Answer A is therefore incorrect.

Road Traffic, para. 3.11.12

11. Driver Licensing

Answer 11.16

Answer **D** — Under s. 96(2) of the Road Traffic Act, 1988, where a constable has reason to suspect that a person may be guilty of driving a motor vehicle on a road with defective eyesight, he or she may require the driver to submit to an eyesight test, which would include the ability to read a registration mark fixed to a motor vehicle from 20.5 metres (or if the registration mark is a new type with narrower characters, 20 metres). (Refusing to do so is an offence under s. 96(3).)

The specific requirements as to eyesight are set out at regs 72–73 and sch. 8 to the Motor Vehicles (Driving Licences) Regulations 1999 (SI 1999 No. 2864). The driver must be given the eyesight test in *good light*, whilst wearing corrective lenses, *if they were worn when the person drove the motor vehicle on a road*. This means that if the person was *not* wearing corrective lenses, they must take the test *without* them. Answers A and C are therefore incorrect. Even if the offence took place in darkness, the driver must take the test in good light. Answers B and C are incorrect for this reason.

Road Traffic, para. 3.11.13.1

12 | Excise and Registration

Please note that the questions in this chapter relate to material in the Blackstone's Police Manuals which has been excluded from the OSPRE® syllabus for 2005.

> **STUDY PREPARATION**
>
> This is another highly practical area. The Vehicles (Crime) Act 2001 has introduced stricter controls on the supply and fitting of registration plates. Further powers under this Act allow police officers to enter motor salvage operators' premises to inspect vehicles.
>
> In addition to these, you need to know the circumstances in which certain vehicles have to display some form of vehicle excise licence; you also need to know which vehicles require registration marks and who will be liable to a criminal penalty if they fail to do so.

QUESTIONS

Question 12.1

Certain vehicles are exempt from having to pay duty under the Vehicle Excise and Registration Act 1994.

In relation to the exemption, which of the following statements is correct?

A Vehicles over 25 years may be exempt, and they may be required to display a 'nil' licence.
B All vehicles over 25 years are exempt, however, they must display a 'nil' licence.
C Vehicles over 25 years may be exempt, however, they must display a 'nil' licence.
D All vehicles over 25 years are exempt, and they may be required to display a 'nil' licence.

139

12. Excise and Registration

Question 12.2

Section 29 of the Vehicle Excise and Registration Act 1994 creates an offence of keeping an unlicensed vehicle on a road.

Who may authorise proceedings for an offence under this section?
- **A** The Secretary of State only.
- **B** The Driver and Vehicle Licensing Agency.
- **C** The Secretary of State or the police.
- **D** The Crown Prosecution Service or the police.

Question 12.3

When a person has been convicted of an offence under s. 29 of the Vehicle Excise and Registration Act 1994 (keeping an unlicensed vehicle on a road), how much duty may the court order that person to pay?
- **A** Only the back duty owed.
- **B** Up to three times the annual duty rate, as well as any back duty owed.
- **C** Up to twice the annual duty rate, as well as any back duty owed.
- **D** Up to five times the annual duty rate, as well as any back duty owed.

Question 12.4

Constable PLATT was on patrol with an officer from the DVLA, searching for unlicensed vehicles, with the intention of clamping them. They received a complaint of an abandoned vehicle, which had been obstructing a driveway for some weeks. The vehicle was not displaying an excise licence, and Constable PLATT arranged for it to be moved around the corner, where it was clamped.

Has Constable PLATT acted in accordance with powers given by the Vehicle Excise Duty (Immobilisation, Removal and Disposal of Vehicles) Regulations 1997 in these circumstances?
- **A** No, the vehicle should not have been moved, it should have been clamped where it was found.
- **B** No, the vehicle should not have been clamped, as it was an abandoned vehicle.
- **C** Yes, the vehicle may be moved to a new location, where it may be clamped.
- **D** No, the vehicle should not have been clamped; it was not displaying an excise licence which had expired.

12. Excise and Registration

Question 12.5

Section 33(1) of the Vehicle Excise and Registration Act 1994 makes it an offence to fail to display a licence when a vehicle is on a road.

Would the prosecution need to prove anything in relation to the defendant's state of mind, when prosecuting this offence?

A Yes, that the defendant was aware of the offence.
B No, the defendant must show he or she had no intent.
C No, it is for the defendant to introduce the statutory defence.
D No, the offence is one of absolute liability.

Question 12.6

Part III of the Road Vehicles (Registration and Licensing) Regulations 2002 deals with the production of a vehicle registration document to a constable or a person acting on behalf of the Secretary of State.

What is the specified period of time allowed for a person to produce such a document?

A The document must be produced within 5 days.
B The document must be produced within 7 days.
C The document must be produced within a reasonable time.
D The document must be produced within 28 days.

Question 12.7

HUMPHRIES owns a car showroom. However, his premises are not large enough to keep all the cars inside. During the daytime, HUMPHRIES parks many of his cars on the road outside. None of the vehicles is taxed and they are returned to the showroom at night. HUMPHRIES has six trade licences and places these on the vehicles when they are parked on the road.

Is HUMPHRIES entitled to keep the vehicles on the road while displaying trade licences in this manner?

A Yes, provided he has a trade licence for each vehicle.
B No, he may not keep the vehicles on the road in these circumstances.
C Yes, provided they are on the road in the course of business.
D Yes, if the vehicles are temporarily in his possession.

12. Excise and Registration

Question 12.8

Constable PENG saw an unattended vehicle parked on a road, not displaying an excise licence. Constable PENG made enquiries to establish the owner's identity, but was unable to do so. Two months later, Constable PENG stopped BOULD driving the vehicle. BOULD stated that he had bought the vehicle from a car dealer recently and was not the owner of it at the time of the offence. The vehicle was now displaying an excise licence.

Is Constable PENG entitled to ask BOULD for details of the previous keeper in these circumstances?

A No, as BOULD was not the keeper of the vehicle at time of the offence.
B Yes, but BOULD may have a defence if he is unable to provide the details.
C Yes, and BOULD would have no defence if he is unable to provide the details.
D No, Constable PENG may only make the enquiry with the dealer who sold the car.

Question 12.9

Who, if either, of the people below would commit an offence under the Road Vehicles (Display of Registration Marks) Regulations 2001 if their vehicle was used on a road?
1. PETERS has a motor vehicle, which was registered on 1 February 2001. The vehicle is fitted with registration plates whose characters are in italic script.
2. LEE owns a motor cycle, which was registered on 1 October 2001. LEE has fixed a number plate to the front and rear of the motor cycle.

A PETERS only.
B LEE only.
C Both.
D Neither.

Question 12.10

KANE owns a garage, which specialises as a body shop for spray painting cars. He instructed one of his workers, HEGG, to park a car on the road while they were awaiting a delivery. The car was not displaying registration plates, as they had been removed for the bodywork to be sprayed. HEGG parked the car outside the premises, and returned it about 20 minutes later.

Who, if anyone, would be guilty of an offence under s. 42(1) of the Vehicle Excise and Registration Act 1994 (failing to display a registration mark) in these circumstances?

12. Excise and Registration

A KANE only, as the keeper of the vehicle.
B HEGG only, as the driver of the vehicle.
C Both people, KANE as the keeper and HEGG as the driver.
D Neither person, as the vehicle was only temporarily on the road.

Question 12.11

Part 2 of the Vehicles (Crime) Act 2001 imposes a statutory duty on a registered supplier of vehicle registration plates to give notice to the Secretary of State, when he or she ceases to carry on his or her business.

When should a registered person submit his or her notification to the Secretary of State?

A Within 28 days before he or she intends ceasing to carry on business.
B The day that he or she ceases to carry on business.
C Within 28 days after he or she ceases to carry on business.
D Within 7 days before he or she intends ceasing to carry on business.

Question 12.12

Sergeant DAY is in charge of a Stolen Vehicle Squad and suspects that a salvage yard operated by FERRY is receiving stolen vehicles on a regular basis. Sergeant DAY intends attending FERRY's yard with another officer from her team to inspect the vehicles on the premises. Both officers will be in plain clothes.

Do the officers have the authority to enter the salvage yard in these circumstances, under the Vehicles (Crime) Act 2001?

A No, the officers would only have the power to enter the premises in order to inspect the register.
B Yes, provided they are able to produce proof of their identity, if required to do so.
C No, they would require a warrant to enter the premises to inspect vehicles in these circumstances.
D Yes, but only if they were accompanied by an officer in uniform, or a person from the local authority.

12. Excise and Registration

ANSWERS

Answer 12.1

Answer **A** — Vehicles over 25 years *may* be exempt from having to pay excise duty, provided they were constructed *before* 1 January 1973.

Exempt vehicles *may* be required to display a 'nil' licence when used on a road.

Answer A is the only correct combination; therefore, answers B, C and D are incorrect.

Road Traffic, para. 3.12.2.2

Answer 12.2

Answer **C** — Proceedings may be brought under s. 29 of the Vehicle Excise and Registration Act 1994 only with the authority of the Secretary of State. The Secretary of State may provide authority for the police to bring proceedings by issuing a certificate of approval to do so (s. 47(4)). Answers A and D are incorrect. The Driver and Vehicle Licensing Agency (DVLA) is responsible for managing the database of drivers' details and answer B is incorrect.

Road Traffic, para. 3.12.2.3

Answer 12.3

Answer **D** — A person committing an offence under s. 29 may be required to pay up to five times the annual duty rate. He or she must also pay back the duty unpaid. Consequently, answers A, B and C are incorrect.

Road Traffic, para. 3.12.2.3

Answer 12.4

Answer **B** — The Vehicle Excise Duty (Immobilisation, Removal and Disposal of Vehicles) Regulations 1997 (SI 1997 No. 2439) empower 'authorised persons', such as the police and the DVLA, to clamp certain vehicles when the authorised person has reason to believe that an offence has been committed under s. 29 of the Vehicle Excise and Registration Act 1994, in relation to that vehicle. The fact that the vehicle is not displaying a licence would give rise to such suspicion and, therefore, answer D is incorrect.

12. Excise and Registration

The vehicle may either be clamped where it is, or be moved to another location and clamped. Answer A is therefore incorrect.

Certain vehicles are exempt from being clamped and abandoned vehicles are included in this list (presumably because there is little prospect of recovering duty from such a vehicle). The vehicle in question *should not* have been dealt with using this power. Therefore, answer B is correct, which means that answer C is incorrect.

Road Traffic, para. 3.12.2.3

Answer 12.5

Answer **D** — The offence is one of absolute liability and the prosecution have no duty to prove a guilty state of mind, even if the licence was removed by another person (*Strowger* v *John* [1974] RTR 124). Answer A is therefore incorrect.

There is no statutory defence, and because the offence is one of absolute liability, there is no provision for the defendant to establish a defence. Answers B and C are therefore incorrect.

Road Traffic, para. 3.12.2.7

Answer 12.6

Answer **C** — Unlike the other main documents which should be produced when a person is issued with an HO/RT/1, the registration document must be produced 'within a reasonable time', rather than within a fixed period of days. Answers A, B and D are therefore incorrect.

Road Traffic, para. 3.12.3

Answer 12.7

Answer **B** — The details for the various obligations placed on trade licence holders are to be found in Part VII of the Road Vehicles (Registration and Licensing) Regulations 2002 (SI 2002 No. 2742). The Regulations contain a list of businesses covered for use of trade licences, including dealing in vehicles. The new Regulations also contain a list of things the holder of the licence must not do (or permit another person to do).

It is still an offence, under s. 34(1)(c) of the Vehicle Excise and Registration Act 1994, to use a trade licence to keep a vehicle on a road in any circumstances other than circumstances which have been prescribed. The fact that he has trade licences for all the vehicles would not allow HUMPHRIES to park vehicles on the road for the purposes described in the question. Answer A is therefore incorrect.

145

12. Excise and Registration

Trade licences *may* be used only in the course of a person's business, but not in these circumstances. Answer C is therefore incorrect.

Lastly, trade licences may be used only on vehicles which are temporarily in a trader's possession, but again, not in these circumstances. Answer D is therefore incorrect.

Road Traffic, para. 3.12.4

Answer 12.8

Answer **B** — The current *keeper* of a vehicle is obliged to provide details of the keeper of the vehicle at the time of the offence, even if that person was not the keeper at that time (s. 46(1)(a) of the Vehicle Excise and Registration Act 1994 and see *Hateley* v *Greenough* [1962] Crim LR 329). Answer A is therefore incorrect.

Section 46(2)(b) of the 1994 Act requires *any other person* to provide such information as is in his power to give as to the identity of the person who kept the vehicle on a road at the time of the offence. This would include asking the car dealer in the scenario but, because of the above, is not restricted to that person. Answer D is therefore incorrect.

There is a statutory defence provided by s. 46(6), if a person charged with an offence is able to satisfy the court that he or she did not know, and could not with reasonable diligence have ascertained, the identity of the person or persons concerned. Answer C is therefore incorrect.

Road Traffic, para. 3.12.5

Answer 12.9

Answer **B** — The circumstances in statement 1 do not amount to an offence under the Road Vehicles (Display of Registration Marks) Regulations 2001. It will be an offence for a vehicle first registered *on or after* 1 September 2001 to be fitted with registration plates whose characters are in italic script. Vehicles registered before this date are not affected (reg. 15).

The circumstances in statement 2 *do* amount to an offence under the above Regulations. Any motor cycle first registered *on or after* 1 September 2001 *must not* be fitted with a registration plate to the front. Vehicles registered before this date *need not* be fitted with such plates (reg. 6).

Consequently, answers A, C and D are incorrect.

Road Traffic, para. 3.12.6.1

12. Excise and Registration

Answer 12.10

Answer **C** — Under s. 42 of the Vehicle Excise and Registration Act 1994, the 'relevant person' commits an offence if he or she 'drives' a vehicle on a road, when it is not displaying a registration mark. HEGG would commit the offence; therefore, answers A and D are incorrect.

Where the vehicle is not being driven, the 'keeper' will commit an offence under this section. A person will be the 'keeper' if he or she causes the vehicle to be on a public road for any period, *however short*, when it is not in use. Therefore, as KANE was responsible for causing the vehicle to be on the road, he also commits the offence. It is irrelevant how long the vehicle was on the road. Answers B and D are therefore incorrect.

Road Traffic, para. 3.12.6.4

Answer 12.11

Answer **C** — A registered person who is not carrying on business as a registration plate supplier must give notice to the Secretary of State of that fact, *within 28 days* of the beginning of the period in which they are not carrying on business while registered (in other words, within the first 28 days after they stop trading). Failure to give notice as required is a summary offence punishable by a fine (s. 27(5) of the Act). Answers A, B and D are therefore incorrect.

Road Traffic, para. 3.12.7.1

Answer 12.12

Answer **B** — The Vehicles (Crime) Act 2001 provides several powers to police officers dealing with salvage businesses. Under s. 9 of the Act, a constable may enter premises at a reasonable time to inspect either the premises itself, or any motor vehicles or salvageable parts. There is no requirement for the constable to be in uniform or to be accompanied by a person from the local authority, therefore answer D is incorrect. If the constable is not in uniform, he or she must be able to produce evidence of his or her identity if required.

A constable may also enter such a premises to inspect the register, but this is in *addition* to the above powers (answer A is therefore incorrect). Lastly, a constable *may* apply for a warrant to enter premises (which would allow the officer to enter by force), but this is not a prerequisite if force is not to be used, therefore, answer C is incorrect.

Road Traffic, para. 3.12.8.3

13 | Goods and Passenger Vehicles

Please note that the questions in this chapter relate to material in the Blackstone's Police Manuals which has been excluded from the OSPRE® syllabus for 2005.

> **STUDY PREPARATION**
>
> In common with several other areas, the law relating to goods and passenger vehicles has been condensed in the *Blackstone's Police Manuals*. Nevertheless, there is still a lot of detail, particularly in terms of the different categories of vehicle (seating, weight etc.).
>
> Operators' licences, drivers' hours and power of enforcement are all key areas of this topic. So too are the laws regulating the licensing and use of taxis.

QUESTIONS

Question 13.1

In relation to the defitions of goods vehicles and passenger carrying vehicles, which of the following statements, if any, is/are correct?
1. A large goods vehicle (LGV) is a motor vehicle for carrying goods, having a maximum permissible weight over 7 tonnes.
2. A large passenger carrying vehicle (PCV) is one for carrying more than 16 passengers.
3. A small passenger carrying vehicle (PCV) is one for carrying more than 12 passengers, but fewer than 16.

A Statements 1 and 2 only.
B All of the above.
C Statements 2 and 3 only.
D Statement 2 only.

13. Goods and Passenger Vehicles

Question 13.2

Regulation 16(8) of the Motor Vehicles (Driving Licences) Regulations 1999 prohibits holders of provisional driving licences from carrying passengers in certain circumstances, when they are driving a passenger carrying vehicle.

In relation to those restrictions, which of the following statements is correct?
A They apply only when a person is undergoing a driving test.
B They apply only to large passenger carrying vehicles.
C They apply only to drivers under 21.
D They apply only when a person is not undergoing a driving test.

Question 13.3

MORRIS is 20 years of age and the holder of a provisional large goods vehicle (LGV) driving licence. MORRIS has appeared in court for an offence of speeding, which takes the number of penalty points on his driving licence to six.

What does reg. 56 of the Motor Vehicles (Driving Licences) Regulations 1999 say in relation to MORRIS being disqualified from holding a LGV licence?
A He must be disqualified if he accumulates 12 penalty points.
B He must be disqualified now.
C He may be disqualified now.
D He must be disqualified if he accumulates *more than* 6 penalty points.

Question 13.4

O'SHEA is employed as a long-distance lorry driver and possesses a large goods vehicle (LGV) licence. He is 51 years of age and his licence is due for renewal.

If O'SHEA renews his licence now, when will he next have to renew it?
A The new licence will last for 5 years.
B The new licence will last until his 66th birthday.
C The new licence has to be renewed annually.
D The new licence will last until his 55th birthday.

Question 13.5

Regulation 50 of the Motor Vehicles (Driving Licences) Regulations 1999 provides that in certain circumstances, a police officer may drive a large passenger-carrying vehicle on a road when not licensed to do so.

13. Goods and Passenger Vehicles

In what circumstances may this power be used?
A When the vehicle is causing an obstruction only.
B When the vehicle is causing an obstruction, or in order to protect life and property.
C When the vehicle is causing an obstruction, or in order to protect life.
D When it is necessary to protect life and property only.

Question 13.6

PARKER wishes to hire a small passenger carrying vehicle (PCV) to take his friends to a football match. The cost of the vehicle is to be shared amongst the friends. PARKER does not have a PCV licence.

In which circumstances may PARKER drive such a vehicle?
A He must be over 18 and have held an ordinary driving licence for at least two years.
B He must be over 21 and have held an ordinary driving licence for at least two years.
C He must be over 21 and have held an ordinary driving licence for at least 12 months.
D He may not drive such a vehicle, as he is not the holder of a PCV licence.

Question 13.7

ALBERT owns a bakery company, which produces its own cakes and bread, and several shops in the local area. All goods produced at the bakery are delivered to his own shops, using 15 vans which are also owned by ALBERT. Each of the vans has a 'plated' weight of 5 tonnes.

Does ALBERT require an operator's licence in these circumstances?
A No, the vehicles are too small.
B Yes, a standard operator's licence.
C Yes, a restricted operator's licence.
D No, the vehicles are not used for hire or reward.

Question 13.8

BASHIR owns the Travel Lodge Hotel, situated near an airport. BASHIR has purchased a small mini bus designed to carry 12 passengers. He intends to offer guests the facil-

13. Goods and Passenger Vehicles

ity of a ride to the airport from his hotel. Guests will not be charged extra for the facility; however, BASHIR has included the journey in the cost of the room.

Does BASHIR's vehicle qualify as a public service vehicle (PSV) in these circumstances?

A   Yes, it is a PSV and BASHIR will need an operator's licence.
B   No, as passengers are not required to pay separate fares.
C   Yes, it is a PSV, but BASHIR will not require an operator's licence.
D   No, because the vehicle is not being used for hire or reward.

Question 13.9

What type of driving licence would you expect a community bus driver to hold?

A   PCV licence and community bus permit.
B   Community bus permit only.
C   PCV licence or community bus permit.
D   PSV licence and community bus permit.

Question 13.10

Part VI of the Transport Act 1968 regulates drivers' hours for certain types of vehicles.

Which of the following vehicles are generally covered by the Act?

A   Passenger carrying vehicles constructed or adapted to carry more than 8 passengers.
B   Passenger carrying vehicles constructed or adapted to carry more than 16 passengers.
C   Passenger carrying vehicles constructed or adapted to carry more than 12 passengers.
D   All public service vehicles, regardless of how many passengers are carried.

Question 13.11

What are the daily and weekly driving hours that are generally acceptable in order to comply with Part VI of the Transport Act 1968?

A   Ten hours daily driving, with no more than 56 hours per week.
B   Eight hours daily driving, with no more than 50 hours per week.

13. Goods and Passenger Vehicles

C Nine hours daily driving, with no more than 56 hours per week.
D Nine hours daily driving, with no more than 40 hours per week.

Question 13.12

In relation to the issue and retention of tachograph record sheets, which of the following statements is correct?

A It is the driver's responsibility to ensure that he or she has enough tachographs; drivers must also ensure that they are kept for at least one year.
B Employers must ensure that sufficient tachographs are issued to each driver, and employers must ensure that they are kept for at least one year.
C It is the driver's responsibility to ensure that he or she has enough tachographs; employers must ensure that they are kept for at least one year.
D Employers must ensure that sufficient tachographs are issued to each driver, and employers must ensure that they are kept for at least two years.

Question 13.13

In relation to the production and submission of tachograph record sheets, which of the following statements is correct?

A Employers must be able to produce drivers' sheets for the current week; drivers must return completed sheets to their employer within 21 days.
B Drivers must be able to produce sheets for the current month; they must also return completed sheets to their employer within 21 days.
C Drivers must be able to produce record sheets for the current week; they must also return completed sheets to their employer within 28 days.
D Drivers must be able to produce record sheets for the current week; they must also return completed sheets to their employer within 21 days.

Question 13.14

Constable UNDERHILL is dealing with a road traffic accident, involving a heavy goods vehicle which drove off without stopping. Constable UNDERHILL visited CLEGG, whose company owns the vehicle. The company is based in the UK. Constable UNDERHILL requested from CLEGG the tachograph record sheet relating to the vehicle on the day of the accident.

What power would be available to Constable UNDERHILL if CLEGG refused to produce the required document?

13. Goods and Passenger Vehicles

A Stop the vehicle being driven on a road until the required document is produced.
B Stop the vehicle being driven on a road and direct it to be removed to a police station until the document is produced.
C Report CLEGG for obstruction and stop the vehicle being driven on the road until the document is produced.
D Detain the vehicle in question until the document is produced.

Question 13.15

Which body (outside the Metropolitan and London police areas) has the responsibility for providing a licensing system for hackney carriages to ply for hire as taxis?

A The local authority.
B The magistrates' court.
C The police.
D The Secretary of State.

Question 13.16

WILLIS has bought a vehicle, which she intends to use as a hackney carriage. WILLIS intends to ply for taxi fares in two neighbouring districts in the South West of England. One area is a busy shopping centre, where she would work in the daytime; the other area is located near a number of night clubs, where she would work in the evening. However, the two districts are controlled by separate licensing bodies.

How many licences should WILLIS apply for, in order to work in the two districts?

A WILLIS may hold only one licence and she may only work in one district.
B WILLIS requires two licences, one for each district.
C WILLIS may hold only one licence, but each district she works in will be named on the licence.
D WILLIS may hold only one licence, but there are no restrictions on where she works.

Question 13.17

In what circumstances would an authority be able to refuse an application by a taxi driver for a licence to ply for hire?

A If the applicant has failed to convince the authority that he or she is a fit and proper person, on the balance of probabilities.

13. Goods and Passenger Vehicles

B If the applicant has failed to convince the authority that he or she is a fit and proper person, beyond reasonable doubt.
C The police must convince the authority that he or she is not a fit and proper person, on the balance of probabilities.
D The police must convince the authority that he or she is not a fit and proper person, beyond reasonable doubt.

Question 13.18

If a vehicle is licensed as a hackney carriage in one district, can it also be licensed as a private hire vehicle in another district?

A Yes, but only in the neighbouring district.
B Yes, in any other district.
C No, vehicles licensed as hackney carriages cannot be licensed as private hire vehicles.
D No, they may only be licensed as such in the same district.

Question 13.19

STIRLING has recently had his hackney carriage licence revoked when it was due for renewal, as he was not a fit and proper person. STIRLING lived next door to a public house, where many of the customers had used his services in the past. One busy Saturday night, STIRLING sat in his taxi on his driveway, which was in full view of the public house, at closing time, hoping that when people came out, they would approach him asking for a taxi ride home.

Has STIRLING committed an offence of plying for hire without a licence in these circumstances?

A Yes, but only if he is approached by a customer.
B No, he would need to make some positive move towards the people.
C Yes, the offence is complete in these circumstances alone.
D No, he is not plying for hire on a road or in a public place.

13. Goods and Passenger Vehicles

ANSWERS

Answer 13.1

Answer **D** — Statement 1 is incorrect; a large goods vehicle (LGV) is a motor vehicle used for carrying goods, having a maximum permissible weight over 7.5 tonnes.

Statement 2 is correct; a large passenger carrying vehicle (PCV) is one which is used for carrying more than 16 passengers.

Statement 3 is incorrect; a small passenger carrying vehicle (PCV) is one which is used for carrying more than 8 passengers, but fewer than 16.

Consequently, answers A, B and C are incorrect.

Road Traffic, paras 3.13.2.1, 3.13.2.2

Answer 13.2

Answer **D** — Under the Motor Vehicles (Driving Licences) Regulations 1999 (SI 1999 No. 2864), the holder of a passenger carrying vehicle provisional driving licence must not carry passengers other than a supervising qualified driver or a full licence holder who is giving/receiving instruction. These restrictions *do not* apply during a driving test. Answer A is therefore incorrect.

The restrictions apply to the use of any passenger carrying vehicles by provisional driving licence holders, not just large PCVs. Answer B is therefore incorrect. They also apply to any provisional licence holder and not just persons under 21. Answer C is therefore incorrect.

Road Traffic, para. 3.13.3

Answer 13.3

Answer **B** — Under reg. 56 of the Motor Vehicles (Driving Licences) Regulations 1999, if the holder of a large goods vehicle (LGV) licence is under 21 years of age and he or she accumulates more than *three* penalty points (or is disqualified), that person *must* be disqualified from holding a LGV licence. Answers A, C and D are incorrect for this reason.

Road Traffic, para. 3.13.3.1

13. Goods and Passenger Vehicles

Answer 13.4

Answer **A** — The rules governing the renewal of large goods vehicle (LGV) and passenger carrying vehicle (PCV) licences can be found in s. 99(1A)(a) of the Road Traffic Act 1988. First, a driver's licence will last until his or her 45th birthday, or for 5 years, whichever is the *longer* (in other words, a person aged 21 will not have to renew his or her licence until his or her 45th birthday). However, where the person is aged between 45 and 65, the licence will last for 5 years, or until the person's 66th birthday, whichever is the *shorter*. This means that the driver in the scenario will have to renew his licence in 5 years, this being the shorter period. Answers B, C and D are incorrect for this reason.

Road Traffic, para. 13.3.3.1

Answer 13.5

Answer **B** — Under reg. 50 of the Motor Vehicles (Driving Licences) Regulations 1999, a police officer will be exempt from Part IV and may drive a passenger-carrying vehicle on a road when not licensed to do so. The power may be exercised *either* when the vehicle is causing an obstruction to other road users or members of the public, *or* in order to protect life and property. Since answer B is the only one which covers all the requirements, answers A, C and D are incorrect. (Note that there is no requirement for the officer to be in uniform in order to exercise this power).

Road Traffic, para. 3.13.3.2

Answer 13.6

Answer **B** — A person who is not the holder of a passenger carrying vehicle (PCV) licence may drive a small PCV without a full PCV licence for social purposes, other than for hire or reward and on behalf of a non-commercial body (reg. 7 of the Motor Vehicles (Driving Licences) Regulations 1999). Since the hirer of the vehicle meets these requirements, answer D is incorrect.

Further conditions are imposed on a driver of a small PCV in the above circumstances. The person must be over 21 years of age, and have held an ordinary driving licence for at least *two* years. Answers A and C are therefore incorrect.

Road Traffic, para. 3.13.3.2

13. Goods and Passenger Vehicles

Answer 13.7

Answer **C** — There are two types of operator's licences — 'standard' and 'restricted'. A restricted licence will be required for a person who is using vehicles solely in connection with his or her own trade or business *other than the carriage of goods for hire or reward*. Since the person in the scenario is carrying his *own* goods, he requires a restricted licence. Answer B is therefore incorrect. Answer D is incorrect for the same reason.

An operator's licence is *not* required if the vehicles being used are small goods vehicles, which are vehicles with a plated weight of 3.5 tonnes or less. The vehicles in the scenario are 5 tonnes; therefore an operator's licence is required. Answer A is therefore incorrect.

Road Traffic, paras 3.13.4.2, 3.13.4.5

Answer 13.8

Answer **A** — Under s. 1 of the Public Passenger Vehicles Act 1981, a public service vehicle (PSV) is:

(1) a motor vehicle (other than a tramcar) which —
 (a) being a vehicle adapted to carry more than eight passengers, is used for carrying passengers for hire or reward; or
 (b) being a vehicle not so adapted, is used for carrying passengers for hire or reward at separate fares in the course of a business of carrying passengers.

The vehicle in the scenario is designed to carry more than eight passengers; therefore, to qualify as a public service vehicle (PSV) you would have to prove that passengers were being carried for hire or reward (under s. 1(1)(a) above). Hotel courtesy buses have been held to be PSVs on the basis that the service was part of the overall hotel 'service', the cost of which was included in the price of a room or meal (*Rout v Swallow Hotels Ltd* [1993] RTR 80). This mirrors the scenario given and therefore answer D is incorrect.

There is no need to prove that the vehicle was being used for carrying passengers at separate fares (under s. 1(1)(b)), as the vehicle is designed to carry more than eight passengers and qualifies as a PSV under s. 1(1)(a). Answer B is therefore incorrect. All PSVs being used on a road for hire or reward require an operator's licence, irrespective of the type of service provided (s. 12). Answer C is therefore incorrect.

Road Traffic, para. 3.13.5

13. Goods and Passenger Vehicles

Answer 13.9

Answer **C** — Under the Community Bus Regulations 1978 and 1986, drivers of a community bus *may* hold a community bus permit which *exempts* them from the need for a passenger carrying vehicle (PCV) licence. This means that the driver may hold *either* a community bus permit, or a PCV licence. Answers A and B are incorrect. Community buses are provided for the social and welfare needs of communities, which means that they are *not* operating for hire or reward. This, in turn, means that the driver does not need a public service vehicle (PSV) licence, and answer D is incorrect.

Road Traffic, para. 3.13.9.1

Answer 13.10

Answer **C** — Part VI of the Transport Act 1968 generally applies to passenger service vehicles (PSVs) and other motor vehicles constructed or adapted to carry more than 12 passengers. Answers A and B are therefore incorrect.

There are exemptions for vehicles that are not required to carry passengers for long distances, normally those controlled by public authorities. Not all PSV drivers are restricted by the rules; therefore answer D is incorrect.

Road Traffic, para. 3.13.10.1

Answer 13.11

Answer **C** — Under Part VI of the Transport Act 1968, the acceptable hours are normally a nine-hour daily driving period, with a ten-hour period no more than twice a week. The total period of driving for any one week must not exceed 56 hours (or 90 hours per fortnight). Answers A, B and D are therefore incorrect.

Road Traffic, para. 3.13.10.3

Answer 13.12

Answer **B** — It is the employer's duty to ensure that all drivers working for them have sufficient tachographs. The drivers have the responsibility to ensure that the tachos are in use when they drive the vehicles. Answers A and C are therefore incorrect.

Employers must also ensure that tachograph sheets are retained for at least *one* year, for inspection on request of an authorised inspector. Answers A and D are incorrect for this reason.

Road Traffic, para. 3.13.10.4

13. Goods and Passenger Vehicles

Answer 13.13

Answer **D** — Under the Community Recording Equipment Regulations, *drivers* must be able to produce tachograph record sheets for the current *week* (and also for the last day of the previous week they drove). Answers A and B are therefore incorrect.

Drivers must also return completed sheets to their employer within 21 days. Answer C is incorrect for this reason.

Road Traffic, para. 3.13.10.4

Answer 13.14

Answer **D** — Under s. 99(1) of the Transport Act 1968, a constable (or authorised person) may require any person to produce and permit him or her to examine and copy any record sheet that that person is required to retain or be able to produce. For the purpose of exercising the power, the constable/authorised person may detain the vehicle during such time as is required for the exercise of the power.

If the *driver* of a vehicle obstructs a constable or fails to comply with a requirement made, the constable (or authorised person) may prohibit the person from driving the vehicle on a road. The constable/authorised person may also direct the vehicle to a place specified by him or her. Since the constable in the question was dealing with the owner and not the driver, this second power is not applicable and answer A is therefore incorrect.

An officer exercising the power above could direct the vehicle to any place, not just a police station. However, again this power applies when dealing with the driver of a vehicle and therefore answer B is incorrect.

A person failing to comply with any requirement to allow inspection of records would commit a specific offence under s. 99 of the 1968 Act and therefore could be reported for that offence and not obstruction. Answer C is therefore incorrect.

Road Traffic, para. 3.13.10.5

Answer 13.15

Answer **A** — Under s. 37 of the Town Police Clauses Act 1847, local authorities have the responsibility for providing a licensing system for hackney carriages to ply for hire as taxis. Answers B, C and D are therefore incorrect.

Note: In London the system for hackney carriages and private hire vehicles is provided under the Metropolitan Public Carriage Act 1869. The licensing authority is Transport for London.

Road Traffic, para. 3.13.11.1

13. Goods and Passenger Vehicles

Answer 13.16

Answer **B** — Under the Local Government (Miscellaneous Provisions) Act 1976, all hackney carriage licences are issued by a particular district. Therefore, in order to ply for hire in more than one district, a hackney carriage driver would have to apply for one licence for each district. There appears to be no limit on the number of licences a person may apply for. Answers A, C and D are incorrect for this reason.

Road Traffic, para. 3.13.11.1

Answer 13.17

Answer **A** — If an authority refuses a person's hackney carriage licence, the decision may be based on the civil law standard of proof — 'balance of probabilities' (see *R v Maidstone Crown Court, ex parte Olson* [1992] *The Times*, 21 May). Answers B and D are incorrect.

In arriving at its decision, the authority *may consult* with the local police for advice, but the onus is on the applicant to convince the authority that he or she is a fit and proper person. Answer C is therefore incorrect.

Road Traffic, para. 3.13.11.2

Answer 13.18

Answer **B** — A vehicle licensed as a hackney carriage in one district *may* be licensed as a private hire vehicle in another district (*Kingston-upon-Hull Council* v *Wilson* [1995] *The Times*, 25 July). Answers A, C and D are therefore incorrect.

Road Traffic, para. 3.13.11.1

Answer 13.19

Answer **C** — It is a summary offence to operate, drive or ply for hire without the relevant licence. The Divisional Court held that 'plying for hire' can extend to a situation where the vehicle is in a prominent position on private property just off a street when the public was there in numbers (*Eastbourne Borough Council* v *Stirling* [2001] RTR 65). Answer D is therefore incorrect.

A taxi driver may be 'plying for hire' simply by being parked in a prominent position. There is no requirement to prove that the defendant made some positive move towards the public, or even that he or she was actually approached by a customer. Answers A and B are therefore incorrect.

Road Traffic, para. 3.13.11.3

14 | Fixed Penalty System

Please note that the questions in this chapter relate to material in the Blackstone's Police Manuals which has been excluded from the OSPRE® Inspectors' Exam syllabus for 2005.

> **STUDY PREPARATION**
>
> The fixed penalty notice (FPN) system is pretty straightforward. Understand the principles behind it and you will realise that the system is simply designed to speed up the administration of some common offences which won't result in disqualification.
>
> The flowcharts in the *Blackstone's Road Traffic Manual* are useful in seeing the whole system at work.

QUESTIONS

Question 14.1

Which of the following statements, if either, is/are correct in relation to the fixed penalty procedure under the Road Traffic Offenders Act 1988?
1. A fixed penalty may not be issued, where the offence is one of causing or permitting an offence specified in the schedule.
2. Where the offence committed does not involve an obligatory endorsement, a fixed penalty may only be issued in relation to a stationary vehicle.

A Statement 1 only.
B Statement 2 only.
C Both statements.
D Neither statement.

Question 14.2

RICHIE was stopped by Constable WELLER for a speeding offence. Constable WELLER intended issuing RICHIE with a fixed penalty notice for the offence. RICHIE did not

14. Fixed Penalty System

have his driving licence with him, but stated that there were some points on it, although he could not remember how many.

Under what circumstances could RICHIE be made to surrender his driving licence for the offence, if he produces it within seven days?

A None, as he did not have it with him at the time, he should be reported for the offence.
B He must produce it to a constable or authorised person, provided he is not likely to exceed 11 points for this offence.
C He must produce it to a constable in uniform, provided he is not likely to exceed 12 points for this offence.
D He must produce it to a constable or authorised person, provided he is not likely to exceed 12 points for this offence.

Question 14.3

Where a person has failed to pay a fixed penalty notice during the enforcement period, the police are entitled to ask the court for an increase in the amount payable for the notice.

What increase are the police allowed to ask for in these circumstances?

A Equal to twice the amount of the original notice.
B Equal to 1.5 times the amount of the original notice.
C Equal to three times the amount of the original notice.
D Equal to five times the amount of the original notice.

Question 14.4

SAGGERS was sent a letter by the Clerk to the Justices in his area that a vehicle registered to him has been issued with a fixed penalty notice, and that the notice had not been paid. The letter stated that the police intended asking the court to increase the sum payable on the fixed penalty notice. SAGGERS had sold the vehicle recently to a neighbour, but had forgotten to notify the DVLA. His intention was to return the notice to the Clerk, declaring that he was not the person given the fixed penalty notice.

What period of time is allowed for SAGGERS to return such a declaration to the court?

A Within 21 days from the time the notice was sent by the Clerk.
B Within 14 days of receiving the notice from the Clerk.

14. Fixed Penalty System

C Within 14 days from the time the notice was sent from the Clerk.
D Within 21 days of receiving the notice from the Clerk.

Question 14.5

Under the Functions of Traffic Wardens (Amendment) Order 1986, traffic wardens are given certain powers to issue fixed penalty notices.

What kind of fixed penalty notices may a traffic warden issue?
A Both non-endorsable and endorsable, for any offence.
B Non-endorsable only, for certain offences only.
C Both non-endorsable and endorsable, but only for certain offences.
D Non-endorsable for all offences; endorsable for certain offences only.

Question 14.6

Section 75(8)(1)(a) of the Road Traffic Offenders Act 1988 specifies a period during which a person issued with a conditional offer of a fixed penalty may make a payment in order to avoid attending court.

What is the length of the specified period?
A 14 days.
B 21 days.
C One month.
D 28 days.

Question 14.7

SANCHEZ was driving on a road with a 30 mph speed limit, when she activated a speed camera at 45 mph. SANCHEZ was sent a conditional offer of a fixed penalty notice, which she duly returned, together with her driving licence and payment for the offence. The administrating office noticed that SANCHEZ already had points on her driving licence and, taking into account the new offence, she would now be liable for disqualification.

What should the administrating office now do with SANCHEZ's driving licence and payment for the offence?
A Forward the payment to the court and the driving licence to the police.
B Forward both the payment and the driving licence to the court.

14. Fixed Penalty System

C Return the payment to SANCHEZ and forward the driving licence to the court.
D Return both the payment and the driving licence to SANCHEZ and notify the police.

14. Fixed Penalty System

ANSWERS

Answer 14.1

Answer **C** — Statement 1 is correct; s. 51(2) of the Road Traffic Offenders Act 1988 specifies that a person may be issued only with a fixed penalty notice (FPN) if the offence relates to the 'use' of the vehicle on a road. The system does not apply to those who 'cause' or 'permit' the use of a vehicle on a road while an offence is being committed.

Statement 2 is also correct; s. 62(1) of the Road Traffic Offenders Act 1988 allows a constable to affix a notice to a *stationary* vehicle. The purpose of s. 62(1) is to enable a non-endorsable FPN to be issued where the driver is not present. Presumably the legislators envisaged practical problems with attempting to affix such a notice to a moving vehicle!

Consequently, answers A, B and D are incorrect.

Road Traffic, paras 3.14.3, 3.14.4.2

Answer 14.2

Answer **B** — A person may be issued with a fixed penalty notice (FPN) if he or she commits an offence to which the procedure applies (in this case, an endorsable offence). The person may not be issued with a FPN if he or she would be liable for disqualification if convicted for the offence. A person would be disqualified under the 'totting up' procedure if his or her driving licence shows *12 points* or more. Answer D is incorrect as a FPN may be issued only if the points are likely to *exceed* 11 points, not 12.

If a person does not have his or her licence at the time of the offence, he or she may be required to produce it within seven days and therefore answer A is incorrect. There is a safeguard built in here, because if it is discovered at this stage that the penalty points are likely to reach 12 points, the driving licence will not be surrendered.

Lastly, the driving licence may be produced either to a constable in uniform *or* to an authorised person, such as an enquiry clerk at a police station. Answer C is therefore incorrect.

Road Traffic, para. 3.14.4.1

14. Fixed Penalty System

Answer 14.3

Answer **B** — If the person has not paid a fixed penalty, or given notice requesting a court hearing by the end of the enforcement period, the police can register a sum equal to *1.5* times the amount of the penalty for enforcement against that person (s. 55(3) of the Road Traffic Offenders Act 1988). Answers A, C and D are therefore incorrect.

Road Traffic, para. 3.14.4.1

Answer 14.4

Answer **D** — If a person receives a notice stating that a fixed penalty notice (FPN) has not been paid, he or she may serve a statutory declaration to the court to the effect either that he or she was not the person who was given the FPN, or that he or she has given a notice requesting a court hearing. In either case, the statutory notice must be made and served within *21 days of receiving the notice from the clerk* (and not 21 days from the time the notice was sent). Answers A, B and C are therefore incorrect.

Road Traffic, para. 3.14.4.1

Answer 14.5

Answer **C** — Under the Functions of Traffic Wardens (Amendment) Order 1986 (SI 1986/1328) a traffic warden has the same powers as a constable to issue fixed penalty notices (FPNs), for *both* endorsable and non-endorsable offences. Answer B is incorrect. Traffic wardens may issue FPNs of both types, *for certain offences only*, therefore, answers A and D are incorrect.

Road Traffic, para. 3.14.4.2

Answer 14.6

Answer **D** — Under s. 75(8)(a) of the Road Traffic Offenders Act 1988, the specified period is 28 days and therefore answers A, B and C are incorrect.

Road Traffic, para. 3.14.5

14. Fixed Penalty System

Answer 14.7

Answer **D** — Under s. 76(4) of the Road Traffic Offenders Act 1988, where a person is sent a conditional offer of a fixed penalty notice (FPN), and that person is liable for disqualification, the payment and the licence will be returned to the *defendant* and the police will be notified. This would give the police the opportunity to proceed by way of summons. Consequently, answers A, B and C are incorrect.

Road Traffic, para. 3.14.5

15 | Pedal Cycles

Please note that the questions in this chapter relate to material in the Blackstone's Police Manuals which has been excluded from the OSPRE® syllabus for 2005.

> **STUDY PREPARATION**
>
> There's not *that* much you can — or can't — do with a bike. Therefore, there's not that much a trainer or examiner can do with a bike question . . .

QUESTIONS

Question 15.1

What is the minimum age at which a person may ride an electrically assisted pedal cycle on a road?

- A   15 years.
- B   16 years.
- C   14 years.
- D   17 years.

Question 15.2

What is the maximum speed at which an electrically assisted pedal cycle may be ridden on a road?

- A   15 miles per hour.
- B   20 miles per hour.
- C   30 miles per hour.
- D   25 miles per hour.

Question 15.3

How many braking systems must be fitted on a either a fixed wheel or a free wheel pedal cycle made on or after 1 August 1984?

15. Pedal Cycles

A On a fixed wheel cycle, two; on a free wheel cycle, one.
B One or two systems on either cycle.
C Two systems on both cycles.
D On a fixed wheel cycle, one; on a free wheel cycle, two.

Question 15.4

LARA was involved in an accident one evening, whilst riding his pedal cycle home from work. At the time, he was riding on a road when an elderly man stepped out from the pavement. LARA was unable to swerve to avoid the pedestrian and collided with him. The pedestrian fell to the ground, and struck his head on the pavement. He was taken to the hospital, where he later died. Three days later, Constable AMBROSE, who was dealing with the accident, attended LARA's home address intending to examine the braking system attached to the pedal cycle.

Would Constable AMBROSE be entitled to enter LARA's home, in order to examine the pedal cycle under the Pedal Cycles (Construction and Use) Regulations 1983?

A No, there is only a power to examine cycles on a road, which he should have done at the time of the accident.
B Yes, and the officer may use force to gain entry if necessary.
C Yes, but only with the permission of the owner of the premises.
D No, the officer should have attended within 48 hours of the accident.

Question 15.5

OWEN had been drinking for most of the day in a pub situated in a pedestrian precinct and left in a drunken state. OWEN had his pedal cycle with him, but felt too drunk to ride it. He pushed it along the busy precinct, bumping into people as he went. Constable WEAVER was passing by and witnessed the behaviour.

What action may Constable WEAVER take in respect of OWEN under the Road Traffic Act 1988?

A None, as OWEN is not on a road.
B Arrest OWEN for being in charge of a cycle whilst drunk.
C Report OWEN for being in charge of a cycle whilst drunk.
D None, as OWEN is not riding the cycle.

15. Pedal Cycles

Question 15.6

Section 31(1) of the Road Traffic Act 1988 places a requirement for cycle races on public ways to be authorised before they take place.

Of the people listed below, who may commit an offence in relation to a cycle race which is not authorised?

A   A person advertising the race, promoting or taking part in it.
B   A person promoting the race or taking part in it.
C   A person promoting the race, taking part in it or spectating.
D   A person promoting the race only.

15. Pedal Cycles

ANSWERS

Answer 15.1

Answer **C** — Under s. 32 of the Road Traffic Act 1988, the minimum age at which a person may ride an electrically assisted pedal cycle on a road is 14 years and therefore answers A, B and D are incorrect.

Road Traffic, para. 3.15.2.1

Answer 15.2

Answer **A** — Under the Pedal Cycles (Construction and Use) Regulations 1983, the maximum speed at which an electrically assisted pedal cycle may be ridden on a road is 15 miles per hour and therefore answers B, C and D are incorrect.

Road Traffic, para. 3.15.2.1

Answer 15.3

Answer **D** — Under the Pedal Cycles (Construction and Use) Regulations 1983 (SI 1983 No. 1176), a pedal cycle made on or after 1 August 1984 must comply with the following:

- On a free wheel cycle, two independent braking systems: one acts on the front wheel and one on the rear.
- On a fixed wheel cycle, one braking system acting on the front wheel.

Answer D is the only correct combination and therefore answers A, B and C are incorrect.

Road Traffic, para. 3.15.2.2

Answer 15.4

Answer **D** — Under reg. 11 of the Pedal Cycles (Construction and Use) Regulations 1983, a constable in *uniform* may test a pedal cycle to ensure that the braking system conforms with the Regulations. The constable has the power to do so either when the pedal cycle is on a road, or following an accident. Since this may be done in either of these circumstances, answer A is incorrect. If the pedal cycle has been involved in an accident, the constable may enter any premises to examine it, *provided he or she does*

15. Pedal Cycles

so within 48 hours of the accident, and the owner of the premises consents. Answer C is incorrect, as the officer in the scenario attended *more than* 48 hours after the accident. There is no mention in the Regulations of being able to use force in order to conduct the test, therefore answer B is incorrect.

Road Traffic, para. 3.15.2.2

Answer 15.5

Answer **D** — A person commits an offence under s. 30 of the Road Traffic Act 1988 if he or she *rides* a cycle on a road or public place when unfit to ride it through drink or drugs. There is no mention of being 'in charge' for an offence under this section. Answers B and C are therefore both incorrect.

Had the person been riding the cycle, he would have committed an offence, as the offence may occur in a public place. Answer A is therefore incorrect. Further, there is no power of arrest for an offence under the section. Answer B would still have been incorrect.

An offence may also be committed in these circumstances under s. 12 of the Licensing Act 1872 (but *not* under the Road Traffic Act 1988), of being in charge of a carriage in a public place while drunk.

Road Traffic, para. 3.15.3

Answer 15.6

Answer **B** — The offence under s. 31(1) of the Road Traffic Act 1988 is committed by the person either promoting the race or taking part in it, when the race or speed trial was not authorised. Answers A, C and D are therefore incorrect.

Road Traffic, para. 3.15.4

16 Forgery and Falsification of Documents

Please note that the questions in this chapter relate to material in the Blackstone's Police Manuals which has been excluded from the OSPRE® Inspectors' Exam syllabus for 2005.

> **STUDY PREPARATION**
>
> The end of the road — or at least road traffic.
>
> There are relatively few offences involving forgery and falsification, though as much road traffic law — and its enforcement — relies upon records, these offences are more relevant than they may at first appear.

QUESTIONS

Question 16.1

UNION was stopped while driving PIPER's car on a road and was asked to produce his driving documents. UNION did not have his own policy of insurance. PIPER did not have insurance either, as he had failed to keep up his monthly payments and his insurance company had cancelled the policy. PIPER was still in possession of the insurance certificate, and he lent this to UNION for him to produce it. UNION was aware of the situation when he produced the documents.

Have either UNION or PIPER committed the offence of forgery of documents under s. 173 of the Road Traffic Act 1988?

A Yes, UNION only commits this offence in these circumstances.
B Yes, UNION and PIPER both commit this offence in these circumstances.
C Yes, PIPER only commits this offence in these circumstances.
D Yes, UNION commits this offence; PIPER is guilty of aiding and abetting.

173

16. Forgery and Falsification of Documents

Question 16.2

What power of arrest, if any, would a constable be able to rely on, where a person has committed an offence of making a false statement to obtain a certificate of insurance?

A   The constable may arrest the person for an arrestable offence.
B   No power of arrest, the constable may proceed by summons only.
C   Any constable may arrest any person found committing the offence.
D   A constable in uniform may arrest any person found committing the offence.

Question 16.3

Section 174 of the Road Traffic Act 1988 deals with the offence of making false statements and withholding information.

What would the prosecution need to show in order to prove an offence under this section?

A   The offence is one of specific intent, and the prosecution must show that the defendant gained from the transaction.
B   There is no need for the prosecution to prove intent, or that the defendant gained from the transaction.
C   The offence is one of specific intent, but there is no need to show the defendant gained from the transaction.
D   There is no need to prove intent, but the prosecution must show the defendant gained from the transaction.

16. Forgery and Falsification of Documents

ANSWERS

Answer 16.1

Answer **B** — Under s. 173(1)(b) of the Road Traffic Act 1988, a person commits an offence if, with intent to deceive, he or she lends to, or allows to be used by any other person, a document or other thing to which the section applies. Certificates of insurance are covered, and where a person produced a certificate of insurance issued under a policy which had expired, the offence is made out (*R* v *Cleghorn* [1938] 3 All ER 398). Therefore, PIPER is guilty of the full offence, by lending/allowing UNION to use the insurance certificate.

Under s. 173(1)(a) of the Road Traffic Act 1988 a person is guilty of an offence if, with intent to deceive, he or she 'uses' a document to which this section applies. UNION is guilty of 'using' the document when he produces it. Answers A, C and D are therefore incorrect.

Road Traffic, para. 3.16.2.1

Answer 16.2

Answer **A** — There is a specific offence under s. 174(5)(b) of the Road Traffic Act 1988, of making a false statement to obtain a certificate of insurance. The offence is triable either way and it is an arrestable offence. Answers B, C and D are therefore incorrect.

Road Traffic, para. 3.16.2.2

Answer 16.3

Answer **C** — The offence under s. 174 of the Road Traffic Act 1988 is one of specific intent; therefore answers B and D are incorrect.

There is no need to show that the person actually gained anything or brought about the desired consequences (see *Jones* v *Meatyard* [1939] 1 All ER 140). Answers A and D are incorrect for this reason.

Road Traffic, para. 3.16.2.2

Question Checklist

The checklist below is designed to help you keep track of your progress when answering the multiple-choice questions. If you fill this in after one attempt at each question, you will be able to check how many you have got right and which questions you need to revisit a second time.

	First attempt Correct (✓)	Second attempt Correct (✓)
1 Classifications and Concepts		
1.1		
1.2		
1.3		
1.4		
1.5		
1.6		
1.7		
1.8		
1.9		
1.10		
1.11		
1.12		
1.13		
1.14		
1.15		
1.16		
1.17		
1.18		
1.19		
1.20		
1.21		
1.22		

	First attempt Correct (✓)	Second attempt Correct (✓)
1.23		
1.24		
2 Offences Involving Standards of Driving		
2.1		
2.2		
2.3		
2.4		
2.5		
2.6		
2.7		
2.8		
2.9		
2.10		
2.11		
2.12		
2.13		
2.14		
2.15		
2.16		
2.17		
2.18		
2.19		

Question Checklist

	First attempt Correct (✓)	Second attempt Correct (✓)
3 Notices of Intended Prosecution		
3.1		
3.2		
3.3		
3.4		
3.5		
3.6		
4 Accidents and Collisions		
4.1		
4.2		
4.3		
4.4		
4.5		
4.6		
4.7		
5 Drink Driving		
5.1		
5.2		
5.3		
5.4		
5.5		
5.6		
5.7		
5.8		
5.9		
5.10		
5.11		
5.12		
5.13		
5.14		
5.15		
5.16		
5.17		
5.18		

	First attempt Correct (✓)	Second attempt Correct (✓)
5.19		
5.20		
5.21		
5.22		
5.23		
5.24		
5.25		
5.26		
5.27		
5.28		
5.29		
5.30		
5.31		
5.32		
5.33		
5.34		
6 Insurance		
6.1		
6.2		
6.3		
6.4		
6.5		
6.6		
6.7		
6.8		
7 Safety Measures		
7.1		
7.2		
7.3		
7.4		
7.5		
7.6		
7.7		
7.8		
7.9		

Question Checklist

	First attempt Correct (✓)	Second attempt Correct (✓)
8 Other Measures Affecting Safety		
8.1		
8.2		
8.3		
8.4		
8.5		
8.6		
8.7		
8.8		
8.9		
8.10		
8.11		
8.12		
8.13		
8.14		
8.15		
8.16		
9 Construction and Use		
9.1		
9.2		
9.3		
9.4		
9.5		
9.6		
9.7		
9.8		
9.9		
9.10		
9.11		
9.12		
10 Traffic Signs and Directions		
10.1		
10.2		
10.3		
10.4		

	First attempt Correct (✓)	Second attempt Correct (✓)
10.5		
10.6		
11 Driver Licensing		
11.1		
11.2		
11.3		
11.4		
11.5		
11.6		
11.7		
11.8		
11.9		
11.10		
11.11		
11.12		
11.13		
11.14		
11.15		
11.16		
12 Excise and Registration		
12.1		
12.2		
12.3		
12.4		
12.5		
12.6		
12.7		
12.8		
12.9		
12.10		
12.11		
12.12		
13 Goods and Passenger Vehicles		
13.1		
13.2		

Question Checklist

	First attempt Correct (✓)	Second attempt Correct (✓)
13.3		
13.4		
13.5		
13.6		
13.7		
13.8		
13.9		
13.10		
13.11		
13.12		
13.13		
13.14		
13.15		
13.16		
13.17		
13.18		
13.19		

14 Fixed Penalty System

	First attempt Correct (✓)	Second attempt Correct (✓)
14.1		
14.2		

	First attempt Correct (✓)	Second attempt Correct (✓)
14.3		
14.4		
14.5		
14.6		
14.7		

15 Pedal Cycles

	First attempt Correct (✓)	Second attempt Correct (✓)
15.1		
15.2		
15.3		
15.4		
15.5		
15.6		

16 Forgery and Falsification of Documents

	First attempt Correct (✓)	Second attempt Correct (✓)
16.1		
16.2		
16.3		